# THE HEINZ COOKBOOK

*100 delicious recipes made with
all your favourite ingredients*

# CONTENTS

# FOREWORD

For generations now, in kitchens all over the world, people have created warming and nutritious meals for their loved ones with a little help from Heinz. But as well as enjoying a classic plate of Beanz on toast or serving up meals with a dollop of ketchup for dipping (my granny, for one, knew that a bit of Heinz Tomato Ketchup was a sure way to get me to eat my greens!), creative cooks have long enjoyed using Heinz products as essential ingredients in a whole range of family recipes.

It's something I enjoy doing in my own kitchen, where I make a mean chilli con carne with Heinz Beanz, and I know it gives my kids the same sense of delight I used to feel when my favourite ketchup bottle appeared beside my plate.

Heinz brings joy and comfort to our table, and to many tables the world over. These products have been part of family kitchens for more than 150 years, ever since the young Henry J. Heinz launched his very first variety back in 1869. I wonder if even the visionary Mr Heinz would have dreamed that people would still be cooking up tasty concoctions with his products today, and finding fun and delicious ways to incorporate the best of Heinz into their mealtimes.

This is why I am delighted for us to bring you this selection of brand new and innovative ways to let Heinz help you at mealtimes, providing new recipe ideas and inspiration to help get your creative juices flowing in the kitchen. Some of my favourites, which I cannot wait to try at home with my own family, include the Spiced Sweet Potato & Beanz Quesadillas (page 69), which are sure to be a hit with my kids, and the Halloumi & Courgette Burgers (page 139), which will be perfect for a sunny day.

Everybody at Heinz hopes you enjoy the recipes in this book, whether you're cooking for one or 57. We also love hearing from you and seeing your homemade Heinz recipes, so please do share your creations with us at @heinz_UK (Instagram) and @HeinzUK (Twitter).

*Jojo de Noronha, mum,*
*Beanz chilli chef extraordinaire*
*& Northern Europe President at Heinz*

# BRUNCH

If breakfast is the most important meal of the day, brunch is the most brilliant. It's more creative, more exciting, more varied – just *more*. In this chapter, we've put together a fab collection of brunch favourites, each with its own Heinzy spin. From Cheat's Eggs Royale (with even the hollandaise sauce made outrageously easy) to American Pancakes, there are heaps of treats to enjoy. There's even a Vegan Full English, which is sure to delight plant-based eaters – and surprise omnivores!

# BEANZ & CHORIZO SHAKSHUKA

2 tbsp olive oil

225g chorizo, peeled and
  sliced

2 onions, finely sliced

2 peppers (any colour), finely
  sliced

2 large garlic cloves, crushed

1 tbsp hot smoked paprika

**400g tin Heinz Cream of
  Tomato Soup**

**415g tin Heinz Beanz**

salt and pepper

4 large free-range eggs

small handful of parsley,
  roughly chopped (stalks
  and all)

toasted pitta bread, to serve

Heat the oil in a large, high-sided frying pan (for which you have a lid) over a medium–high heat. Add the chorizo, onions and peppers. Fry, stirring regularly, for 10 minutes until the vegetables have collapsed and softened and the chorizo has released its oils.

Stir in the garlic and paprika and cook, stirring, for 30 seconds, then tip in the tomato soup and baked beans. Give everything a good mix, then let it simmer away for 10 minutes. Season to taste.

Using the back of a spoon, make four wells in the bean and tomato mixture. Crack an egg into each well. Cover the pan with a lid and cook for 2–3 minutes until the egg whites have just set but the yolks are still runny.

Sprinkle over the parsley and serve by placing the pan on a heatproof mat or board in the middle of the table, with toasted pitta bread for scooping.

# CHEAT'S EGGS ROYALE

1 tsp white wine vinegar
4 medium free-range eggs
  (the fresher, the better)
2 English muffins, halved
1 tbsp unsalted butter
4 slices of sustainably
  sourced smoked salmon
small handful of dill, leaves
  picked

*For the cheat's hollandaise*
**4 tbsp Heinz [Seriously
  Good] Mayonnaise**
**2 tsp Heinz Mild Yellow
  Mustard**
zest and juice of ½ lemon
1 tbsp warm water
salt and pepper

To make the cheat's hollandaise, mix together the mayonnaise and mustard in a small bowl. Add the lemon zest and juice, along with the warm water. Season to taste.

Fill a large, deep saucepan with water and place it over a medium heat. Once the water is simmering, add the white wine vinegar. Crack each egg into a separate cup, then, very gently, holding the cup as close to the water as possible, tip the eggs into the water.

Poach the eggs for 2 minutes. During this time, keep an eye on the heat: the water should be simmering rather than spluttering. To check the eggs are done, remove one with a slotted spoon: if the white is still a little wobbly, cook for a few seconds more. Once cooked to your liking, remove the eggs with a slotted spoon and set aside on a plate.

Toast and butter the muffins, then top each muffin half with a slice of smoked salmon and a poached egg. Spoon over the cheat's hollandaise and scatter over some dill leaves to serve.

*To make this into a Cheat's Eggs Florentine, replace the salmon with 200g baby leaf spinach. Fry the spinach in 1 tablespoon of butter with 2 crushed garlic cloves until wilted, then season with salt and pepper to taste.*

SERVES 4

VEGETARIAN

PREP
5 MINUTES

COOK
10 MINUTES

# EASY HUEVOS RANCHEROS

**2 x 390g tins Heinz Fiery Chilli Beanz**
2 tsp ground cumin
2 tbsp olive oil
4 large free-range eggs
salt and pepper
juice of ½ lime
4 small corn tortillas
2 avocados, sliced
100g feta, crumbled
handful of coriander, roughly chopped (stalks and all)

Tip the chilli beans into a saucepan over a medium heat. Add the ground cumin and simmer away for a few minutes.

Meanwhile, pour the olive oil into a large frying pan over a medium–high heat. Crack in the eggs and fry to your liking. Season with a little salt and pepper, then set aside.

Returning to the beans, use a potato masher to roughly mash them, then squeeze in the lime juice.

Heat the tortillas according to the packet instructions, then set out four plates and place a tortilla on each one. Top with the beans, followed by the fried eggs and avocado slices. Scatter over the feta and coriander, and serve.

SERVES 2

VEGETARIAN

PREP
10 MINUTES

COOK
5 MINUTES

# JALAPEÑO SCRAMBLED EGGS

198g tin sweetcorn, drained

100g cherry tomatoes, halved

6–8 pickled jalapeño slices (depending on how spicy you like it), finely chopped, plus 2 tbsp pickling juice from the jar

small handful of coriander, roughly chopped (stalks and all)

**2 tsp + 1 tbsp Heinz Tomato Ketchup**

salt and pepper

6 medium free-range eggs

30g butter

2 tsp cumin seeds

4 spring onions, finely sliced

In a small bowl, mix together the sweetcorn and cherry tomatoes, along with half the pickled jalapeños and half the coriander. Add the jalapeño pickle juice and the 2 teaspoons of ketchup. Stir and season to taste. This is your salsa.

Crack the eggs into a jug. Whisk well with a fork until fully combined. Add the remaining tablespoon of ketchup, along with the remaining pickled jalapeños, and mix well.

Melt the butter in a frying pan over a medium heat. Add the cumin seeds and most of the spring onions. Cook, stirring, for 1–2 minutes until the spring onions have softened, then pour in the egg mixture.

Stir the eggs, moving your spoon through the entire pan every 20 seconds or so until you end up with big pieces of silky scrambled eggs.

Divide the scrambled eggs between two plates. Spoon the salsa next to the eggs, then scatter over the remaining spring onions and coriander to serve.

# SWEET POTATO & AVO TORTILLA

SERVES 4

VEGAN

PREP
10 MINUTES

COOK
10 MINUTES

2 sweet potatoes, peeled and
  cut into chunks
2 limes, halved
2 avocados, sliced
salt and pepper
4 large tortilla wraps
**4 tbsp Heinz [Seriously
Good] Vegan Chilli
Mayonnaise**
4 handfuls of rocket
2 roasted peppers from a jar,
  drained and sliced

Put the sweet potatoes and one of the halved limes in a microwaveable bowl. Cover, then microwave on high for 10 minutes until the potatoes are completely soft.

Meanwhile, in a small bowl, use a fork to smash the avocados. Squeeze in the juice from the remaining lime, mix well, and season with salt and pepper to taste.

Carefully uncover the microwaved sweet potatoes. Squeeze over the juice from the microwaved lime, then use a potato masher to roughly mash. Season to taste.

Using scissors, cut a slit from one edge of each tortilla wrap to the middle at the 'three o'clock' position, then divide the different fillings equally between the four quarters of each tortilla wrap, as shown in the photo overleaf: spread the vegan chilli mayonnaise over the lower right-hand quarters and top with a handful of rocket. Gently crush the avocado slices over the top right-hand quarters. Place the peppers on the top left-hand quarters, then spread the mashed sweet potatoes on the bottom left-hand quarters.

Fold the first quarter of the wrap over the second, then fold the second quarter over the third. Finally, fold the third quarter over the last to encase the filling in a triangular wrap, and serve.

*Pictured overleaf.*

SERVES 2

VEGAN

PREP
5 MINUTES

COOK
15 MINUTES

# VEGAN FULL ENGLISH

3 tbsp olive oil
200g cherry tomatoes on
  the vine
salt and pepper
200g button mushrooms,
  any larger ones halved
300g silken tofu
1 tbsp Cajun seasoning
**415g tin Heinz Beanz**
2 garlic cloves, crushed
small handful of parsley,
  chopped (stalks and all)

*To serve*
toast
**Heinz [Seriously Good]
  Vegan Mayonnaise and/or
  Heinz Tomato Ketchup**

Heat 2 tablespoons of the olive oil in a large frying pan over a high heat. Add the cherry tomatoes to one side of the pan. Season with salt and pepper and leave to soften. Tip the button mushrooms into the other side of the pan. Cook, stirring the mushrooms occasionally, for 4–5 minutes until golden brown.

Meanwhile, heat the remaining tablespoon of olive oil in another frying pan over a medium heat. Add the silken tofu and, using a spoon, break up the tofu into small pieces so it resembles scrambled eggs. Add the Cajun seasoning and stir to combine. Season, then leave to simmer away while you finish the rest of the breakfast.

Heat the beans in a small saucepan over a medium heat for 3–4 minutes until hot.

Next, add the garlic to the mushrooms and stir. Cook for a final 30 seconds, then sprinkle over the parsley and take off the heat.

Drain any liquid that has come from the tofu and then divide the scramble between two plates, followed by the garlicky mushrooms, tomatoes and beans. Serve with toast, vegan mayonnaise and/or ketchup.

# TRUFFLE ROSTI WITH EGGS & GREEN VEG

SERVES 2

VEGETARIAN

PREP
5 MINUTES

COOK
20 MINUTES

350g floury potatoes (we like Maris Piper or King Edwards), peeled and coarsely grated

**3 tbsp Heinz [Seriously Good] Truffle Mayonnaise**

salt and pepper

2 tbsp olive oil

2 large free-range eggs

200g asparagus tips, halved

100g frozen peas

Place the grated potatoes in the middle of a clean tea towel, then gather up the sides of the towel to make a bundle. Holding it over the sink, squeeze as much water out of the potatoes as you can, then tip the squeezed potatoes into a large bowl. Stir through 2 tablespoons of the truffle mayonnaise and season well with salt and pepper.

Heat the olive oil in a large frying pan over a medium heat. Using clean hands, scoop up a quarter of the potato mixture and shape into a rough round about 1cm thick. Carefully lay this rosti in the pan, then repeat with the remaining mixture until you have four rostis. Fry the rostis for 4–5 minutes on each side until deep golden brown and cooked through. Keep warm.

Meanwhile, bring a saucepan of water to the boil, then carefully drop the eggs into the boiling water. Set a timer for 4 minutes. Once the timer beeps, add the asparagus and frozen peas to the same saucepan and boil for another 2½ minutes.

Drain the eggs, asparagus and peas in a sieve. Remove the eggs and run under cold water until cool enough to handle, then peel and halve.

Divide the rostis between two plates and spread them with the remaining tablespoon of truffle mayonnaise. Top with the asparagus, peas and halved boiled eggs.

SERVES 4

VEGETARIAN
OPTION

PREP
15 MINUTES

COOK
25 MINUTES

# TATTIE SCONES WITH BACON & BEANZ

500g floury potatoes (we like Maris Piper or King Edwards), peeled and halved

50g salted butter, plus 1 tbsp for cooking

salt and black pepper

100g self-raising flour, plus extra for dusting

small handful of chives, snipped (optional)

12 rashers of streaky bacon

**2 x 415g tins Heinz Beanz**

*You will need a rolling pin*

Put the potatoes in a large saucepan of cold salted water. Bring to the boil, then cook for about 15 minutes until completely tender. Drain, then leave to steam dry for a few minutes.

Tip the cooked potatoes into a large bowl and add the 50g butter, along with plenty of salt and pepper. Mash well with a potato masher. Add the flour and chives, if using, then mix everything together to form a smooth dough. Set aside to cool for 5 minutes.

Tip the cooled dough out on to a floured surface. Roll into a circle slightly smaller than the base of your largest non-stick frying pan, then use a sharp knife to cut the dough into eight triangles.

Melt the 1 tablespoon of butter in your frying pan over a medium heat, then add the triangular scones, snugly fitting them into the pan. Cook for 3–4 minutes on each side until evenly golden brown.

Meanwhile, preheat the grill to high and line a grill pan or baking tray with kitchen foil. Lay the bacon slices on the pan or tray. Grill for 2–4 minutes on each side.

At the same time, heat the beans in a small saucepan over a medium heat for 3–4 minutes until hot.

When everything is ready, divide the scones between four plates, along with the bacon and beans, and serve.

*To make this veggie, swap out the bacon for 300g sliced chestnut mushrooms fried in 2 tablespoons of butter until deep golden brown, and sprinkle over a few more chives, if you like.*

# COURGETTE & SWEETCORN FRITTERS

SERVES 4

VEGETARIAN

PREP
10 MINUTES

COOK
15 MINUTES

2 courgettes, coarsely grated

325g tin sweetcorn, drained

zest of 1 lime and juice of 1½,
   plus lime wedges to serve

handful of coriander, roughly
   chopped (stalks and all)

100g self-raising flour

**2 tbsp Heinz Thai Style
Sweet Chilli Sauce, plus
extra to serve**

salt and pepper

2 medium free-range eggs

2 tbsp olive oil

2 ripe avocados, sliced

Place the grated courgette in the middle of a clean tea towel, then gather up the sides of the towel to make a bundle. Holding it over the sink, squeeze as much moisture out of the courgettes as you can, then tip the squeezed courgettes into a large bowl.

Add the sweetcorn, lime zest and most of the chopped coriander, along with the flour, sweet chilli sauce and a good pinch of salt and pepper. Crack in the eggs, then beat together with a wooden spoon to form your fritter batter.

Heat 1 tablespoon of the olive oil in a large non-stick frying pan over a medium heat. Dollop four separate ladlefuls of batter into the pan to make four fritters: this will use up half of your batter. Fry for 2–3 minutes on each side until evenly golden brown and cooked through. Transfer to a plate and keep warm while you fry the rest of the fritters in the remaining oil.

Meanwhile, using a fork, smash the avocados in a small bowl with the lime juice. Season with salt and pepper to taste.

Divide the fritters between four plates. Top with the smashed avocado and sprinkle over the remaining coriander. Serve with some more chilli sauce and lime wedges for squeezing.

*These are great served with a fried egg on top.*

SERVES 2

VEGETARIAN

PREP
5 MINUTES

COOK
5 MINUTES

# TURKISH EGGS

50g unsalted butter

1 large garlic clove, crushed

**2 tbsp Heinz Tomato Ketchup**

1 tsp white wine vinegar

4 medium free-range eggs
(the fresher, the better)

150g Greek yoghurt

salt and pepper

small handful of mixed fresh
herbs (we like basil, dill and
parsley leaves)

2 tbsp pumpkin seeds,
toasted

toasted flatbreads, to serve

Melt the butter in a small frying pan over a medium heat. Once melted, add the garlic and cook for 30 seconds, stirring, then mix in the tomato ketchup and stir until smooth. Keep warm.

Fill a large, deep saucepan with water and place it over a medium heat. Once the water is simmering, add the white wine vinegar. Crack each egg into a separate cup, then, very gently, holding the cups as close to the water as possible, tip the eggs into the water.

Poach the eggs for 2 minutes. During this time, keep an eye on the heat: the water should be simmering rather than spluttering. To check the eggs are done, remove one with a slotted spoon: if the white is still a little wobbly cook for a few seconds more. Once cooked to your liking, remove the eggs with a slotted spoon and set aside on a plate.

Spread the yoghurt across two plates. Top with the poached eggs and a good pinch of salt and pepper, then spoon over the garlic and tomato butter. Scatter over the herbs and pumpkin seeds, and serve with toasted flatbreads.

# ITALIAN-STYLE SAUSAGE SANDWICH

SERVES 4

VEGAN OPTION

PREP
5 MINUTES

COOK
15 MINUTES

2 tsp olive oil

8 pork sausages

**2 tbsp Heinz Tomato Ketchup**

1 tbsp balsamic vinegar

4 ciabatta rolls, halved

**4 tbsp Heinz [Seriously Good] Garlic & Caramelised Onion Mayonnaise**

2 large roasted peppers from a jar, drained and sliced

Heat the olive oil in a large frying pan over a medium heat. Add the sausages. Fry, turning occasionally, for 10–12 minutes until evenly golden brown and cooked through.

Add the ketchup and balsamic vinegar to the pan and continue to cook, spooning the ketchup over the sausages, for another minute or so, until each sausage is sticky and nicely glazed. Remove the sausages from the pan and set aside on a plate.

Keep the pan on the heat and, working in two batches, toast the ciabatta rolls in the pan, cut-side down, for 30 seconds until lightly golden.

Spread the garlic and caramelised onion mayonnaise across the bottom half of each roll. Cut the sausages in half lengthways and divide them between the rolls. Top with the roasted peppers to serve.

*Make this vegan by replacing the pork sausages with vegan sausages and the mayonnaise with Heinz [Seriously Good] Vegan Garlic Aioli.*

MAKES 6–8

VEGETARIAN

PREP
15 MINUTES

COOK
15 MINUTES

# CHEDDAR & PICCALILLI SCONES

200g self-raising flour, plus extra for dusting

½ tsp salt

½ tsp cayenne pepper

50g cold unsalted butter, cut into cubes, plus extra to serve

125g extra-mature Cheddar, grated

1 medium free-range egg

75ml whole milk, plus 1 tbsp for glazing

*To serve*

**Heinz Piccalilli Pickle**

honey roast ham (optional – why not try the Honey & Mustard Baked Ham on page 107?)

*You will need a rolling pin and a 6cm round cutter*

Preheat the oven to 200°C/180°C fan/gas mark 6. Line a large baking tray with baking paper.

Stir the flour, salt and cayenne pepper together in a large bowl. Add the butter and use your fingertips to rub it into the flour until the mixture resembles crumbly breadcrumbs. Stir through 100g of the Cheddar.

Crack the egg into a jug and pour in the 75ml milk. Whisk together.

Pour the milk mixture into the dry mixture and use a wooden spoon to bring everything together into a dough.

Tip the dough out on to a floured surface and roll out until it's about 2.5cm thick. Use a 6cm round cutter to firmly stamp out six scones. Pat any leftover dough together to stamp out more scones.

Transfer the scones to the lined baking tray. Brush the tops with the remaining tablespoon of milk and sprinkle over the remaining cheese. Bake in the top of the oven for 15 minutes until well risen and golden.

Serve the scones warm, spread with more butter, the piccalilli and some ham, if you like.

*The scones will keep for 2 days in an airtight container, but are best eaten on the day they are baked. Reheat in a hot oven for 5 minutes before serving. They will also freeze well: defrost thoroughly and reheat to serve.*

# AMERICAN PANCAKES

SERVES 4

VEGETARIAN

PREP
5 MINUTES

COOK
20 MINUTES

200g self-raising flour
1 tsp baking powder
2 tbsp caster sugar
¼ tsp salt
200ml whole milk
2 medium free-range eggs
**2 tbsp Heinz [Seriously
Good] Mayonnaise**
3 tsp vegetable oil

*To serve*
Maple syrup, berries, natural
yoghurt, bananas or
whatever you fancy!

In a large bowl, whisk together the flour, baking powder, sugar and salt.

Pour the milk into a jug and crack in the eggs. Add the mayo, then whisk with a fork to combine.

Pour the milk mixture into the dry ingredients, whisking as you go, until you have a completely smooth pancake batter.

Heat 1 teaspoon of the vegetable oil in a large non-stick frying pan over a medium–high heat, tilting the pan to spread the oil around. Use a small ladle to add three dollops of pancake batter to the pan, spacing them apart to keep them separate. Fry the pancakes for 2 minutes until they are puffy and the undersides are golden, then flip and fry for 1–2 minutes on the other side. Transfer to a plate and keep warm while you cook the remaining batter in two more batches using the remaining oil. You should get 12 pancakes in total.

Serve the pancakes with your chosen toppings.

*Pictured overleaf.*

SERVES 12

VEGAN

PREP
15 MINUTES

COOK
25 MINUTES

# VEGAN BLUEBERRY MUFFINS

225g plain flour, plus 1 tbsp for the blueberries

150g caster sugar

2 tsp baking powder

½ tsp salt

240ml unsweetened non-dairy milk (we like soy or almond)

**50g Heinz [Seriously Good] Vegan Mayonnaise**

1 tsp vanilla extract

zest of 1 lemon

150g blueberries (fresh or frozen)

1 tbsp demerara sugar

*You will need a muffin tray and 12 muffin cases*

Preheat the oven to 180°C/160°C fan/gas mark 4 and line a muffin tray with 12 muffin cases.

In a large bowl, whisk together the 225g flour with the sugar, baking powder and salt. Add the non-dairy milk, vegan mayonnaise, vanilla extract and lemon zest. Whisk to combine and form a smooth batter.

In a separate bowl, toss the blueberries in the remaining tablespoon of flour, then fold three quarters of them into the batter.

Spoon the batter evenly between the muffin cases. Top with the remaining blueberries and sprinkle a little demerara sugar over each muffin. Bake for 20–25 minutes until well risen and golden. Serve warm or cold.

*The muffins will keep well for up to 5 days in an air-tight container and can also be frozen: just defrost thoroughly and then refresh in a hot oven for a couple of minutes before serving.*

# CHOCOLATE & WALNUT BANANA BREAD

SERVES 8

VEGETARIAN

PREP
15 MINUTES

COOK
50 MINUTES

sunflower oil, for greasing
**150g Heinz [Seriously Good] Mayonnaise**
2 large free-range eggs
150g soft light brown sugar
3 very ripe banana, peeled and mashed
175g self-raising flour
½ tsp baking powder
¼ tsp salt
50g walnuts, toasted and roughly chopped
100g dark chocolate, chopped

*You will need a 900g loaf tin*

Preheat the oven to 180°C/160°C fan/gas mark 4. Grease a 900g loaf tin with sunflower oil and line the base with baking paper.

In a large bowl, whisk together the mayonnaise and eggs. Add the brown sugar and mashed bananas and whisk to combine, then add the flour, baking powder and salt. Whisk until a smooth cake batter forms, then fold in the walnuts and chocolate.

Tip the batter into your prepared tin. Bake in the centre of the oven for 45–50 minutes until well risen and golden and a skewer inserted into the centre of the loaf comes out clean.

Let the banana bread cool for a few minutes in the tin, then turn out on to a wire rack. Serve warm or allow to cool completely. We like to eat ours toasted and spread with butter.

*This banana bread will keep well in an airtight container for up to a week. It can also be frozen: we suggest slicing it before freezing, so that slices can be toasted straight from frozen to serve.*

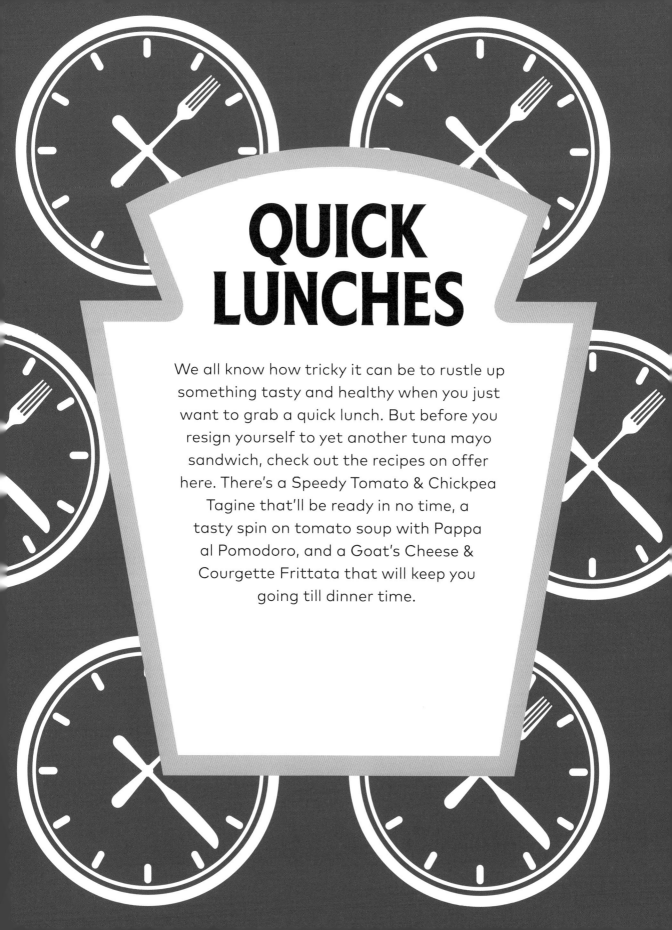

# QUICK LUNCHES

We all know how tricky it can be to rustle up something tasty and healthy when you just want to grab a quick lunch. But before you resign yourself to yet another tuna mayo sandwich, check out the recipes on offer here. There's a Speedy Tomato & Chickpea Tagine that'll be ready in no time, a tasty spin on tomato soup with Pappa al Pomodoro, and a Goat's Cheese & Courgette Frittata that will keep you going till dinner time.

SERVES 2

VEGAN

PREP
10 MINUTES

COOK
5 MINUTES

# GREEN GODDESS SOBA NOODLES

salt and pepper

160g soba noodles

150g frozen podded
edamame beans

1 tbsp sesame oil

1 large ripe avocado, halved

**3 tbsp Heinz [Seriously
Good] Vegan Mayonnaise**

juice of 1 lime

thumb-sized piece of fresh
ginger, peeled and grated

large handful of coriander,
roughly chopped (stalks
and all)

200g radishes, roughly
chopped

large handful of mint, leaves
picked

*You will need a food processor
or blender*

Cook the soba noodles in a pan of salted boiling water, according to the packet instructions. For the last 2 minutes of cooking, add the edamame beans to the pan to heat through. Drain together in a sieve and rinse under cold water until cool, then tip into a large bowl. Drizzle in the sesame oil and toss everything together.

Put one avocado half in a mini food processor or blender, along with the vegan mayo, lime juice, ginger and half of the coriander. Blitz to create a smooth green dressing, and season to taste. Chop the remaining avocado half into cubes.

Add the chopped avocado, radishes, mint and remaining coriander to the noodles. Add the dressing and mix everything together, then divide the noodles between two plates to serve.

# BEETROOT & AIOLI BEANZ BURGERZ

SERVES 2

VEGAN

PREP
10 MINUTES

COOK
25 MINUTES

**2 Heinz Original Beanz Burgerz**

2 seeded burger buns

**2 tbsp Heinz [Seriously Good] Vegan Garlic Aioli**

2 ready-cooked beetroots, sliced into rounds

*For the chopped salad*
½ cucumber

1 small red onion, finely chopped

200g cherry tomatoes, quartered

large handful of parsley, chopped (stalks and all)

juice of ½ lemon

2 tbsp olive oil

big pinch of dried oregano

salt and pepper

Cook the Beanz Burgerz in the oven or under the grill according to the packet instructions.

Meanwhile, make the salad. Use a peeler to peel the outer part of the cucumber into long ribbons. Set these aside, then chop the cucumber core and place in a large bowl. Add the red onion, cherry tomatoes, parsley, lemon juice, olive oil and oregano and mix. Season to taste.

Warm the buns in the oven or under the grill, then slice in half. Spread the vegan garlic aioli across the bottom halves of the buns. Top with the bean burgers, followed by the sliced beetroot and cucumber ribbons, then sandwich together. Serve with the chopped salad.

SERVES 2

VEGAN

PREP
5 MINUTES

COOK
10 MINUTES

# SWEET & SOUR TOFU

3 tbsp cornflour

280g extra-firm tofu,
   cut into cubes

2 tbsp rapeseed oil

1 green pepper, finely sliced

250g pouch pre-cooked
   basmati rice

*For the sweet and sour sauce*

**3 tbsp Heinz Tomato Ketchup**

100ml pineapple juice

1 tbsp soft light brown sugar

1 tbsp soy sauce

3 tbsp rice wine vinegar

2 tsp cornflour

1 tbsp water

Begin by preparing the sweet and sour sauce. In a small saucepan, mix together the ketchup, pineapple juice, sugar, soy and rice wine vinegar. Place over a low heat and bring to a simmer. Leave this sauce to simmer away while you prepare the tofu.

For the tofu, spoon the 3 tablespoons of cornflour on to a large plate. Using clean hands, coat the tofu evenly in the cornflour.

Heat the rapeseed oil in a large frying pan over a high heat. Add the cornflour-coated tofu and green pepper. Fry for around 5 minutes, turning the tofu regularly with tongs, until the tofu is golden and crisp and the peppers have softened slightly.

Meanwhile, return to the sweet and sour sauce. In a small bowl, mix together the remaining 2 teaspoons of cornflour with the water to create a milky paste. Add this paste to the sauce and increase the heat to medium. Let the sauce bubble away for a few minutes until thickened.

Heat the rice according to the packet instructions, then divide between two bowls. Top with the tofu and peppers, then pour over the sweet and sour sauce to serve.

# ASPARAGUS & GRATED EGG SALAD

SERVES 2

VEGETARIAN

PREP
5 MINUTES

COOK
10 MINUTES

salt and pepper

2 medium free-range eggs

250g asparagus spears,
   woody ends snapped off

**2 tbsp Heinz Salad Cream**

2 tbsp sunflower seeds,
   toasted

small handful of parsley,
   leaves picked

toast, to serve

Bring a medium saucepan of salted water to the boil over a medium–high heat. Carefully lower in the eggs and boil for 7½ minutes. Use a slotted spoon to transfer the eggs to a bowl of cold water and leave to cool. Drop the asparagus into the still-boiling water in the pan and cook for 2–3 minutes until just tender. Drain into a sieve.

Lay the asparagus across two plates. Spoon over the salad cream and toss to coat.

Peel the cooled eggs, then, using the fine side of a grater, grate one egg on to each plate, over the asparagus. Season with salt and pepper, then scatter over the toasted seeds and parsley. Serve with toast, for scooping.

SERVES 2

VEGETARIAN

PREP
5 MINUTES

COOK
20 MINUTES

# PAPPA AL POMODORO

2 tbsp olive oil, plus extra to serve

2 fat garlic cloves, crushed

1 tsp dried chilli flakes

**2 x 400g tins Heinz Cream of Tomato & Basil Soup**

2 slices of crusty stale bread, roughly chopped

salt and pepper

small handful of basil, leaves picked

Heat 1 tablespoon of the olive oil in a saucepan over a medium heat. Add the garlic and chilli flakes and cook, stirring, for 30 seconds, then pour in the tomato and basil soup. Bring to a boil, then add the stale bread. Reduce the heat to low and leave the soup to simmer away gently for 15–18 minutes, stirring occasionally, until the bread has mostly broken down and you are left with a thick, textured soup, almost the consistency of porridge. Season to taste.

Stir through the remaining tablespoon of olive oil, then divide between two bowls. Top with the basil leaves, a good crack of black pepper and another drizzle of olive oil to serve.

# VEGAN BANH MI

SERVES 2

VEGAN

PREP
10 MINUTES

COOK
5 MINUTES

2 small baguettes

1½ tbsp cornflour

140g extra-firm tofu, cut into
   cubes

1 tbsp rapeseed oil

**2 tbsp Heinz [Seriously
   Good] Vegan Mayonnaise**

small handful of coriander,
   leaves picked

*For the sauce*

**2 tbsp Heinz Tomato Ketchup**

1 tbsp vegan hot sauce

1 tbsp soy sauce

1 tbsp rice wine vinegar

*For the carrot and cucumber*

1 large carrot, peeled into
   long ribbons

½ cucumber, peeled into long
   ribbons

1 tbsp rice wine vinegar

Preheat the oven to 100°C/80°C fan/gas mark ¼.

To make the sauce, mix together the ketchup, hot sauce, soy sauce and rice wine vinegar in a bowl. Set aside.

In a separate bowl, toss the carrot and cucumber ribbons with the vinegar.

Put the baguettes in the oven to warm.

Spoon the cornflour on to a plate and, using clean hands, coat the tofu evenly in the cornflour.

Heat the rapeseed oil in a frying pan over a high heat. Add the tofu and fry, turning regularly with tongs, for around 5 minutes until golden and crisp, then tip the tofu into the bowl of sauce and stir so that each piece is coated.

Slice the warm baguettes in half, and spread vegan mayonnaise across the bottom halves. Layer on the carrot and cucumber, followed by the sticky tofu and sauce. Top with the coriander and sandwich together with the tops of the baguettes to serve.

SERVES 2

PREP
5 MINUTES

COOK
15 MINUTES

# STICKY SALMON & SWEET POTATO MASH

200g long-stem broccoli

salt and pepper

2 tbsp sesame oil

2 sustainably sourced salmon
fillets (about 120g each)

**3 tbsp Heinz Thai Style
Sweet Chilli Sauce**

1 tbsp sesame seeds

2 sweet potatoes, cut into
chunks (skin left on)

1 lime, halved

Preheat the oven to 200°C/180°C fan/gas mark 6.

Spread the broccoli out on a roasting tray. Season with salt and pepper and drizzle over 1 tablespoon of the sesame oil. Roast for 2 minutes, then add the salmon to the tray. Season and spoon the sweet chilli sauce over everything. Sprinkle over the sesame seeds. Roast for 8–9 minutes until the salmon is cooked but still moist and flakes into large chunks, and the broccoli is just tender.

Meanwhile, place the sweet potatoes and lime halves in a microwaveable bowl. Cover, then microwave on high for 10 minutes until the potatoes are completely soft.

Carefully uncover the bowl, then remove the lime halves and squeeze their juice over the potatoes. Drizzle with the remaining tablespoon of sesame oil, then use a potato masher to roughly mash. Season to taste.

Divide the mash between two plates. Serve with the sweet chilli salmon and broccoli.

# SPEEDY TOMATO & CHICKPEA TAGINE

SERVES 2

VEGETARIAN

PREP
5 MINUTES

COOK
10 MINUTES

1 tbsp olive oil, plus extra to serve

1–1½ tbsp ras el hanout (depending on how spicy you like it)

**350g jar Heinz Tomato & Chilli Pasta Sauce**

400g tin chickpeas, drained

150g mixed vegetable antipasti

zest and juice of ½ lemon

salt and pepper

50g feta, crumbled

2 tbsp pomegranate seeds

small handful of mint leaves

couscous, to serve (optional)

Heat the olive oil in a medium saucepan over a medium heat. Add the ras el hanout and cook, stirring, for 30 seconds, then tip in the tomato and chilli sauce, along with the chickpeas.

Add the mixed vegetable antipasti to the pan and give everything a good stir. Bring to a simmer and let it bubble away for 5 minutes, then add the lemon zest and juice. Season to taste.

Divide the speedy tagine between two bowls. Crumble over the feta and top with the pomegranate seeds and mint leaves. Serve with couscous, if you like.

*Pictured overleaf.*

SERVES 2

VEGETARIAN

PREP
10 MINUTES

COOK
5 MINUTES

# GREEN BEAN & TOMATO SALAD

200g fine green beans, trimmed

200g cherry tomatoes, halved

2 large handfuls of watercress

50g flaked almonds, toasted

*For the dressing*

**2 tsp Heinz Honey Yellow Mustard**

3 tbsp olive oil

1½ tbsp white wine vinegar

salt and pepper

To make the dressing, mix together the mustard, olive oil and vinegar in a large bowl. Season with salt and pepper to taste.

Bring a small saucepan of salted water to the boil over a medium–high heat. Drop in the beans and cook for 3–4 minutes until just tender, then drain.

Tip the warm beans into the bowl with the dressing, and add the tomatoes, watercress and flaked almonds. Toss together so that everything gets nicely coated in the dressing, then divide between two plates to serve.

# BEETROOT & WALNUT LENTILS

SERVES 2

VEGAN

PREP
10 MINUTES

COOK
5 MINUTES

250g pouch pre-cooked
lentils

250g ready-cooked beetroot,
cut into wedges

50g walnuts, toasted

**3 tbsp Heinz [Seriously
Good] Vegan Garlic Aioli**

2 large handfuls of baby
spinach leaves

200g frozen peas, defrosted

zest and juice of ½ lemon

1 tsp dried chilli flakes

salt and pepper

Heat the lentil pouch according to the packet instructions, then tip into a large bowl.

Add all the remaining ingredients, and give everything a good mix to combine. Season to taste and serve.

SERVES 2

VEGETARIAN

PREP
5 MINUTES

COOK
20 MINUTES

# GOAT'S CHEESE & COURGETTE FRITTATA

2 tbsp olive oil

2 courgettes, diagonally
 sliced

salt and pepper

2 large handfuls of kale

6 medium free-range eggs

**2 tbsp Heinz Thai Style
 Sweet Chilli Sauce, plus
 extra to serve**

100g goat's cheese

Preheat the grill to maximum.

Pour 1 tablespoon of the olive oil into an ovenproof frying pan over a high heat. Season the courgettes with salt and pepper, then lay half the slices in the pan. Fry for 3–4 minutes on each side until nicely charred and softened, then transfer to a plate. Repeat with the remaining courgette slices and oil.

Return all the courgette slices to the pan, and reduce the heat to low. Add the kale and leave to wilt for 2 minutes.

Meanwhile, crack the eggs into a jug. Whisk well with a fork, then add the sweet chilli sauce and plenty of salt and pepper. Whisk again to combine.

Pour the eggs over the courgette and kale mixture, then crumble over the goat's cheese. Cook the frittata over a medium heat until the edges begin to set, then slide under the grill for 2–3 minutes until puffed up, golden and set. Serve with more sweet chilli sauce.

# EASY CHICKEN RAMEN

SERVES 2

PREP
5 MINUTES

COOK
10 MINUTES

**400g tin Heinz Cream of Chicken Soup**

1 tbsp white miso

2 tsp soy sauce

thumb-sized piece of fresh ginger, peeled and finely grated

2 nests egg noodles

2 small pak choi, quartered lengthways

198g tin sweetcorn (don't drain)

1 spring onion, finely sliced

crispy chilli oil or sriracha, to serve (optional)

Pour the chicken soup into a large saucepan over a medium heat. Fill the tin with water 1½ times, and add that to the pan too. Whisk in the miso, soy sauce and ginger, and bring to the boil.

Once boiling, drop in the noodles and cook for 2 minutes, then add the pak choi and the sweetcorn, along with the liquid from the sweetcorn tin. Cook for 2–3 minutes until the noodles are cooked and the pak choi is wilted and tender.

Divide the cheat's ramen between two bowls. Top with the sliced spring onion and crispy chilli oil or sriracha, if using, to serve.

SERVES 2

PREP
5 MINUTES

COOK
5 MINUTES

# SALMON, ASPARAGUS & MIXED GRAINS

salt and pepper
100g asparagus tips
100g runner beans, sliced
250g pouch pre-cooked
  mixed grains
**3 tbsp Heinz Salad Cream**
1 tbsp capers
large handful of dill, roughly
  chopped
juice of ½ lemon
2 precooked salmon fillets
  (about 120g each)

Bring a saucepan of salted water to the boil. Drop in the asparagus and runner beans and cook for 2–3 minutes until just tender, then drain. Tip into a large bowl.

Heat the grains according to the packet instructions, then add to the bowl with the greens. Add the salad cream, capers and most of the dill. Mix well to combine, and season with lemon juice, salt and pepper to taste.

Divide the grains between two bowls and flake over the salmon in large pieces. Top with the remaining dill to serve.

# FAMILY FAVOURITES

Ever had a meal so good you've practically licked the plate clean? With Heinz, that's a given. And we've made sure this chapter is packed with ideas that will be sure to please the whole family: a hearty, hoop-y Summer Minestrone with Basil Pesto, a super-tasty Peri-Peri Chicken Traybake, and a Green Primavera Risotto full of veggies and flavour. And if you've got room for something sweet, the Chocolate Chip Cookies have you covered.

SERVES 4

VEGAN

PREP
10 MINUTES

COOK
30 MINUTES

# CHILLI & MISO VEGGIE RICE BOWL

2 red onions, cut into wedges

1 large cauliflower, cut into
large florets and stalk
roughly chopped

2 sweet potatoes, cut into
large chunks (skin left on)

2 peppers (any colour), cut
into large chunks

2 tbsp vegetable oil

**4 tbsp Heinz Made for
Veggiez Chilli & Miso Sauce**

salt and pepper

300g basmati rice

small handful of coriander,
roughly chopped

2 tbsp toasted sesame seeds

1 red chilli, finely sliced

Preheat the oven to 220°C/200°C fan/gas mark 7.

Toss the onions, cauliflower, sweet potatoes and peppers in your largest roasting tray with the vegetable oil, chilli and miso sauce, and a pinch of salt and pepper, then spread out into a single layer so that they roast evenly. (If your roasting tin isn't big enough to arrange the veg in one layer, you can split it between two roasting tins.) Roast for 25–30 minutes until the veg are cooked and a little caramelised, giving it a good shake about halfway through.

Meanwhile, cook the rice according to the packet instructions.

Spoon the rice into four bowls. Top with the roasted vegetables and then scatter over the coriander, sesame seeds and chilli to serve.

*You can mix and match the vegetables depending on what you have in your fridge.*

# SPICED SWEET POTATO & BEANZ QUESADILLAS

SERVES 4

VEGETARIAN

PREP
30 MINUTES

COOK
45 MINUTES

2 sweet potatoes, peeled and
   cut into small chunks
1–2 tbsp Cajun seasoning
   (depending on how spicy
   you like it)
**415g tin Heinz Beanz**
4 spring onions, finely sliced
salt and pepper
4 tsp olive oil
8 flour tortilla wraps
100g baby spinach leaves
100g grated mozzarella
hot sauce, to serve (optional)

*For the coriander yoghurt*
large handful of coriander,
   chopped (stalks and all)
150g natural yoghurt
zest and juice of 1 lime

Preheat the oven to 100°C/80°C fan/gas mark ¼.

Put the sweet potatoes in a large pan of cold salted water over a medium-high heat. Bring to the boil, then cook for about 10 minutes until the potatoes are completely tender and a knife slides into the centre with no resistance.

Meanwhile, make the coriander yoghurt. In a small bowl, mix together the coriander, yoghurt and lime zest. Season with salt, pepper and lime juice, then set aside.

Drain the cooked sweet potato, then tip into a large bowl. Add the Cajun seasoning and mash using a potato masher. Tip in the baked beans and roughly mash the beans into the sweet potato. Stir through the spring onions, and season everything with salt and pepper.

Heat ½ teaspoon of the olive oil in a large non-stick frying pan over a medium heat. Place one tortilla in the pan and spread half of it with about an eighth of the sweet potato and bean mixture. Top with about an eighth of the spinach leaves and mozzarella, then fold the empty half of the wrap over the top.

Fry for 2 minutes, then carefully flip and fry for another 2 minutes on the other side until the wrap is nicely golden and the cheese has melted. Transfer to a baking tray and keep warm in the oven while you repeat with the remaining tortillas and filling, using ½ teaspoon of oil for each quesadilla.

Once all the quesadillas are cooked, cut them into triangles and serve with the coriander yoghurt and some hot sauce, if you like.

SERVES 4

VEGETARIAN
& VEGAN OPTIONS

PREP
15 MINUTES

COOK
25 MINUTES

# SUMMER MINESTRONE WITH BASIL PESTO

2 tbsp olive oil

1 onion, finely chopped

2 celery stalks, finely chopped

1 large courgette, finely chopped

salt and pepper

2 large garlic cloves, crushed

big pinch of dried chilli flakes (optional)

**2 x 400g tins Heinz Spaghetti Hoops**

100g baby spinach leaves

*For the pesto*

50g toasted pine nuts

bunch of basil (stalks and all)

50g Parmesan or vegetarian hard cheese, finely grated, plus extra to serve (optional)

4 tbsp olive oil

4 tbsp water

juice of ½ lemon

*You will need a food processor*

Heat the olive oil in a large saucepan over a medium heat. Add the onion, celery and courgette, along with a pinch of salt. Cook, stirring regularly, for 8–10 minutes until the vegetables are soft.

Add the garlic and chilli flakes, if using. Cook, stirring for 30 seconds, then tip in the spaghetti hoops. Half-fill one of the tins with water, and tip that in too. Leave the minestrone to simmer away for 10 minutes while you make the pesto.

Place all the pesto ingredients in a mini food processor and blitz to form a smooth pesto, adding a little more water if needed in order to make it a drizzle-able consistency. Season to taste.

Stir the spinach into the minestrone, and give it a few moments to wilt, then divide the soup between four bowls. Top with the basil pesto and a good crack of black pepper. Grate over a little more cheese to serve, if you like.

*To make this vegan, replace the cheese in the pesto with 1–2 tablespoons of nutritional yeast.*

SERVES 4

VEGETARIAN

PREP
10 MINUTES

COOK
1 HOUR

# CHUNKY VEG RATATOUILLE

3 tbsp olive oil

1 large onion, chopped

1 large aubergine, cut into chunks

2 courgettes, cut into chunks

2 peppers (any colour), cut into chunks

salt and pepper

3 fat garlic cloves, crushed

a few thyme sprigs

**2 x 400g tins Heinz Cream of Tomato Soup**

**1 tbsp Heinz Tomato Ketchup**

1 tbsp balsamic vinegar

small handful of basil leaves (optional)

garlic bread, to serve

Heat the olive oil in a large, high-sided frying pan over a medium–high heat. Add the onion, aubergine, courgettes and peppers, along with a good pinch of salt. Fry, stirring regularly, for 10 minutes until all the veg has collapsed.

Add the garlic and thyme sprigs and cook, stirring, for another 30 seconds, then pour in the tomato soup. Stir in the ketchup and balsamic vinegar. Bring the ratatouille to a boil, then reduce the heat to low and leave to simmer away for 45 minutes until all the veg is completely soft and the sauce has thickened slightly. Season to taste and remove the thyme sprigs.

Scatter over the basil leaves, if using, and serve with garlic bread.

# SWEET CHILLI FISHCAKES

SERVES 4

PREP
15 MINUTES
PLUS CHILLING

COOK
20 MINUTES

*For the fishcakes*

4 sustainably sourced skinless salmon fillets, roughly chopped

**2 tbsp Heinz Thai Style Sweet Chilli Sauce, plus extra to serve**

**1 tbsp Heinz [Seriously Good] Mayonnaise, plus extra to serve**

2 tsp soy sauce

2 spring onions, roughly chopped

50g panko breadcrumbs

1 lime, zested and then cut into wedges

2 tbsp rapeseed oil

*For the greens*

200g long-stem broccoli, larger florets halved lengthways

200g green beans, halved

2 tsp soy sauce

1 tbsp sesame oil

1 tbsp toasted sesame seeds

*You will need a food processor*

First make the fishcakes. Put half the salmon in a food processor, along with the sweet chilli sauce, mayonnaise, soy sauce and spring onions. Blitz to form a smooth paste, then tip into a large bowl. Add the remaining salmon pieces, along with the breadcrumbs and lime zest, and mix until well combined. Shape into 12 fishcakes, then transfer to two plates, cover and chill for 30 minutes. (You can also do this the morning or the night before and leave covered in the fridge until you're ready to cook.)

Preheat the oven to 200°C/180°C fan/gas mark 4.

Heat 1 tablespoon of the rapeseed oil in a large non-stick frying pan over a medium–high heat. Add six of the fishcakes and fry for 2–3 minutes on each side until deep golden and crisp. Transfer to a baking tray while you fry the second batch.

Once all the fishcakes are fried, pop them in the oven for 5 minutes to cook through.

Meanwhile, bring a saucepan of water to the boil over a medium–high heat. Once the water is boiling, drop in the broccoli and green beans. Cook for 3–4 minutes until just tender, then drain and return to the pan. Add the soy sauce, sesame oil and sesame seeds, and toss together.

Divide the fishcakes and greens between four plates. Serve with the lime wedges and more mayonnaise and sweet chilli sauce, for dipping.

# HOMEMADE FISH GOUJON SARNIES

SERVES 4

PREP
15 MINUTES

COOK
10 MINUTES

*For the goujons*
50g plain flour
salt and pepper
2 medium free-range eggs
100g dried breadcrumbs
4 sustainably sourced white
  fish fillets (about 120g
  each), cut into finger-width
  strips
2 tbsp olive oil

*For the cheat's tartare sauce*
**8 tbsp Heinz Salad Cream**
1 banana shallot, finely
  chopped
small handful of parsley,
  finely chopped (stalks and
  all)
4–6 cornichons, chopped,
  plus 1 tbsp pickling juice
  from the jar

*To serve*
8 thick slices of crusty white
  bread
1 baby gem lettuce, sliced
**Heinz Tomato Ketchup**
  **(optional)**

Preheat the oven to 220°C/200°C fan/gas mark 7 and line a baking tray with baking paper.

Get your fish goujon station ready. Measure the flour into a small bowl and season with a little salt and pepper. Crack the eggs into a second bowl, and whisk together with a fork. Put the breadcrumbs into a third bowl.

Working in batches, first coat the fish strips in the flour, shaking off the excess, then dip them in the egg to coat completely, before finally coating them in the breadcrumbs. Place your goujons on the lined baking tray and repeat until all the goujons are breaded.

Drizzle the olive oil over the goujons and bake for 8–10 minutes until cooked through and crisp.

Meanwhile, make the cheat's tartare sauce. In small bowl, mix together the salad cream, shallot, parsley, cornichons and pickling juice, and season to taste.

To serve, spread most of the tartare sauce over four of the slices of bread, then top with the fish goujons and lettuce. Top the sandwiches with the remaining slices of bread and serve with the remaining tartare and some ketchup, if you like.

# PERI-PERI CHICKEN TRAYBAKE

8 skinless, boneless chicken thighs (about 800g in total)

3 peppers (any colour), cut into large chunks

2 courgettes, cut into large chunks

1 tbsp sweet smoked paprika

2 tbsp olive oil, plus extra to serve

salt and pepper

**2 x 415g tins Heinz Beanz**

2 tbsp peri-peri sauce

60g rocket

pinch of dried chilli flakes (optional)

**Heinz [Seriously Good] Mayonnaise, to serve**

Preheat the oven to 220°C/200°C fan/gas mark 7.

Place the chicken thighs, peppers and courgettes in a large, high-sided roasting tin. Toss with the paprika, olive oil and plenty of salt and pepper, then spread out into a single layer so that everything roasts evenly. Roast for 20 minutes.

Transfer the chicken to a plate and add the beans and peri-peri sauce to the roasting tin. Give everything a good stir and then nestle the chicken among the beans. Return to the oven for another 15–20 minutes until the chicken is cooked through, the veg is soft and the sauce is reduced.

Scatter over the rocket, along with a sprinkling of chilli flakes, if you like, and drizzle over a little more olive oil. Bring the tin to the table for people to help themselves, and serve with mayonnaise.

SERVES 4

VEGETARIAN

PREP
15 MINUTES

COOK
25 MINUTES

# TOMATO & MASCARPONE PASTA BAKE

2 tbsp olive oil

1 onion, finely chopped

salt and pepper

3 fat garlic cloves, crushed

**2 x 400g tins Heinz Cream of Tomato Soup**

**1 tbsp Heinz Tomato Ketchup**

big splash of balsamic vinegar

400g large conchiglie pasta shells

200g baby leaf spinach

small bunch of basil, leaves picked

100g mascarpone

125g mozzarella ball, torn

Preheat the oven to 200°C/180°C fan/gas mark 6.

Heat 1 tablespoon of the olive oil in your largest saucepan over a medium heat. Add the onion, along with a pinch of salt. Cook for 8–10 minutes, stirring regularly, until softened but not coloured. Add the garlic and cook, stirring, for 30 seconds, then pour in the tomato soup. Half-fill one of the tins with water, and add that too. Stir in the ketchup and balsamic vinegar, then reduce the heat to low and leave the sauce to gently simmer away while you cook the pasta.

Bring a large pan of salted water to the boil. Drop in the pasta shells and cook for 1 minute less than instructed on the packet. Drain and tip into a medium-sized round baking dish.

Add the spinach to the tomato sauce, along with most of the basil leaves and the mascarpone. Stir until the sauce is creamy and the spinach is wilted. Season to taste.

Spoon the sauce over the pasta shells, then scatter the mozzarella over the top. Drizzle with the remaining olive oil and bake for 15–20 minutes until the top is golden and bubbling.

Scatter over the remaining basil leaves and leave to sit for a couple of minutes before serving at the table for people to help themselves.

# GREEN PRIMAVERA RISOTTO

SERVES 4

VEGETARIAN

PREP
10 MINUTES

COOK
40 MINUTES

2 tbsp olive oil, plus extra to serve

1 large onion, finely chopped

3 fat garlic cloves, crushed

300g arborio rice

250ml white wine

1 litre hot vegetable stock

200g frozen peas

200g asparagus tips, cut into thirds

**400g carton Heinz Soup of the Day Green Garden Vegetables**

salt and pepper

juice of ½ lemon

100g feta, crumbled

handful of mint leaves

Heat the olive oil in a large, high-sided frying pan over a medium heat. Add the onion and fry, stirring regularly, for 8–10 minutes until soft but not coloured. Add the garlic and cook, stirring, for 30 seconds more, then tip in the rice.

Stir to coat the rice in the onion and oil. Let it toast in the pan for 1 minute, then pour in the wine. Cook, stirring regularly, until the wine has been absorbed, then add a ladleful of vegetable stock. Continue to cook, still stirring regularly, until the stock has been absorbed, then repeat. Keep adding the stock until it has all been absorbed and the rice is tender, with a slight bite – this will take about 20 minutes.

Add the peas, asparagus and soup to the pan. Give everything a good mix, then cook for 2–3 minutes until the asparagus is just tender.

Season the risotto with salt, pepper and lemon juice to taste, then divide between four bowls. Crumble over the feta, tear over the mint leaves and drizzle over a little more olive oil before serving.

*Pictured overleaf.*

# [SERIOUSLY GOOD] CALAMARI

SERVES 4

PREP
15 MINUTES

COOK
10 MINUTES

300ml buttermilk
2 tsp smoked paprika
1 tsp garlic granules
½ tsp cayenne pepper
   (optional)
salt and pepper
400g frozen sustainably
   sourced squid tubes,
   defrosted and sliced into
   5mm-thick pieces
150g plain flour
150g cornflour
vegetable oil, for shallow-
   frying

*To serve*
**Heinz [Seriously Good]**
   **Mayonnaise**
1 lemon, cut into wedges

*You will need a digital
   thermometer, if you
   have one*

In a large bowl, whisk together the buttermilk, paprika, garlic granules and cayenne (if using), along with plenty of salt and pepper. Drop in the squid pieces and toss well to coat.

In a separate bowl, whisk together the plain flour and cornflour, and line a baking tray with paper towels.

Place a deep frying pan over a high heat and add enough vegetable oil to give a depth of about 2.5cm. Heat the oil to 180°C, using a digital thermometer to check the temperature. Alternatively, you can check if the oil is ready for frying by dropping a crumb of bread into the pan: it should brown within 20 seconds.

Once the oil is up to temperature, dredge about a third of the buttermilk-coated squid in the flour mixture, making sure it is fully coated, then carefully lower it into the oil. Fry for 2 minutes until deeply golden and crisp. Remove with a slotted spoon and place on the lined tray, then repeat with the remaining squid in two more batches.

Once all the calamari have been fried, sprinkle over a little salt and lots of black pepper. Serve the calamari piled up on a plate, with mayonnaise on the side and lemon wedges for squeezing over.

*If you can get fresh, prepared squid from a fishmonger, this recipe will be even more delicious!*

SERVES 4

VEGAN

PREP
10 MINUTES

COOK
45 MINUTES

# ROASTED VEG VEGAN CHILLI

2 peppers (any colour), cut into large chunks

1 small butternut squash, peeled, deseeded and cut into large chunks

2 red onions, cut into wedges

1 large aubergine, cut into large chunks

2 tbsp ground cumin

salt and pepper

4 tbsp olive oil

1 garlic bulb, halved horizontally

**2 x 390g tins Heinz Fiery Chilli Beanz**

330g tomato passata

1 tsp hot smoked paprika

1 tbsp balsamic vinegar

*To serve*

cooked rice

coconut yoghurt

chopped coriander (stalks and all)

Preheat the oven to 220°C/200°C fan/gas mark 7.

Combine the peppers, butternut squash, red onions and aubergine in your largest deep roasting tin. Toss with the cumin, plenty of salt and pepper and the olive oil, then spread out into a single layer so that they roast evenly. (If your roasting tin isn't big enough to arrange the veg in one layer, you can split it between two roasting tins for this part.) Nestle the halved garlic bulb among the veg, then roast for 30 minutes until all the vegetables are completely soft, giving it a shake halfway.

If you split your veg between two trays for the first stage, now you'll need to combine in whichever tray is biggest and deepest. Squeeze the garlic out of its papery skins, then add the chilli beans, passata, paprika and balsamic vinegar. Give everything a good mix, then return to the oven for another 15 minutes.

Serve the vegan chilli with cooked rice, coconut yoghurt and coriander.

*This chilli is even more delicious reheated the next day.*

# CHORIZO & PRAWN JAMBALAYA

SERVES 4

PREP
10 MINUTES

COOK
50 MINUTES

2 tbsp olive oil

110g chorizo, peeled and sliced

1 large onion, finely chopped

2 celery stalks, finely sliced

salt and pepper

2 red peppers, finely sliced

2 fat garlic cloves, crushed

1–2 tbsp Cajun seasoning (depending on how spicy you like it)

250g long-grain rice

600ml chicken stock

**400g tin Heinz Cream of Tomato with a Kick of Chilli Soup**

165g sustainably sourced raw king prawns

handful of parsley, roughly chopped (stalks and all)

1 lemon, cut into wedges

Heat the olive oil in a large, high-sided frying pan (for which you have a lid) over a medium–high heat. Add the chorizo, onion and celery, along with a pinch of salt. Cook, stirring regularly, for 12–15 minutes until the veg is soft and beginning to caramelise and the chorizo has released its oils.

Stir the peppers into the pan, followed by the garlic and the Cajun seasoning. Cook, stirring, for 1 minute, then tip in the rice. Give everything a good mix so that the rice gets nicely coated in the veggies, then pour in the chicken stock and the soup.

Bring the jambalaya to a simmer, then cover and cook for 20–25 minutes, stirring halfway until the rice is cooked through.

Remove the lid and stir through the prawns. Cook for a further 2 minutes until the prawns have turned from grey to completely pink. Season the jambalaya to taste, then scatter over the parsley.

Bring the pan to the table to serve, with the lemon wedges on the side for squeezing.

SERVES 4

VEGETARIAN
OPTION

PREP
10 MINUTES

COOK
50 MINUTES

# AUBERGINE SPAGHETTI PARMIGIANA

3 aubergines, sliced
   lengthways into 1cm slices
salt and pepper
3 tbsp olive oil
**2 x 400g tins Heinz**
   **Spaghetti Hoops**
1 small garlic clove, crushed
¼–½ tsp dried chilli flakes,
   depending on how spicy
   you want it
2 tsp sherry vinegar
250g mozzarella, torn
large handful of basil leaves
30g Parmesan or vegetarian
   hard cheese, finely grated
salad, to serve

Preheat the oven to 200°C/180°C fan/gas mark 6.

Place the aubergine slices in a large bowl. Season well with salt and pepper, then drizzle over the olive oil. Toss to make sure each slice is evenly coated in oil.

Heat a large frying pan over a high heat. Working in batches, lay the aubergine slices in the pan, fry for 2 minutes on each side until softened and beginning to caramelise. Set aside on a plate and repeat until all the aubergine slices are cooked.

Tip the spaghetti hoops into a large bowl and add the garlic, chilli flakes and sherry vinegar. Stir well and season to taste.

To assemble the parmigiana, cover the base of a medium-sized baking dish with about a quarter of the aubergine slices. Spoon over a quarter of the spaghetti hoops mixture, then top with a quarter of the torn mozzarella and a quarter of the basil leaves. Repeat these layers until everything is used up, ending with a layer of mozzarella and basil. Cover with the grated Parmesan or vegetarian alternative.

Bake for 20–25 minutes until bubbling and golden brown. Leave to stand for 5 minutes before serving. We like to serve this with a fresh salad.

# BAKED CHICKEN SCHNITZELS

SERVES 4

PREP
15 MINUTES

COOK
20 MINUTES

4 chicken breasts (about
    150g each)
salt and pepper
**6 tbsp Heinz [Seriously
    Good] Mayonnaise**
**2 tsp Heinz Honey Yellow
    Mustard**
100g panko breadcrumbs
2 tbsp olive oil

*For the salad*
4 tbsp olive oil
2 tbsp balsamic vinegar
**1 tsp Heinz Honey Yellow
    Mustard**
80g mixed watercress,
    spinach and rocket
1 baby gem lettuce, sliced
200g cherry tomatoes,
    halved
1 cucumber, chopped

*You will need a rolling pin*

Preheat the oven to 220°C/200°C fan/gas mark 7 and place a wire rack over a large roasting tray.

Spread out a large piece of baking paper on your work surface. Season one of the chicken breasts with salt and pepper and lay it on top of the baking paper, then cover with a second large sheet of baking paper. Using a rolling pin, bash the chicken breast between the two layers of paper until it is around 1cm thick. Repeat this process with the remaining chicken breasts.

Mix together the mayonnaise and honey mustard in a wide, shallow bowl. Tip the panko breadcrumbs into a second bowl. One at a time, coat the flattened chicken breasts completely in the mustard mayo and then in the breadcrumbs. Once completely breaded, place on top of the wire rack – using a rack will help keep the schnitzels crispy as they roast.

Drizzle the olive oil over the schnitzels, then roast for 18–20 minutes until cooked through and golden brown.

Meanwhile, make the salad. In a large bowl, whisk together the olive oil, balsamic vinegar and honey mustard. Season to taste, then add the salad leaves, sliced baby gem, cherry tomatoes and cucumber, and toss together.

Divide the schnitzels between four plates and serve with the salad.

SERVES 4

PREP
10 MINUTES

COOK
20 MINUTES

# SCAMPI PO BOYS

4 small part-baked
   baguettes
300g frozen scampi
½ iceberg lettuce, shredded
2 large vine tomatoes, sliced
   into rounds
4 gherkins, sliced (optional)

*For the sauce*
**5 tbsp Heinz [Seriously
   Good] Mayonnaise**
**2 tbsp Heinz Tomato Ketchup**
**1 tbsp Heinz Mild Yellow
   Mustard**
1 small garlic clove, crushed
zest and juice of 1 lemon
salt and pepper
few drops of hot sauce
   (optional)

Preheat the oven to 220°C/200°C fan/gas mark 7.

Put the baguettes in a roasting tray and tip the scampi into another. Place in the oven for 15–20 minutes until both are cooked through, the scampi is crisp and the baguettes are golden.

Meanwhile, make the sauce. In a bowl, mix together the mayonnaise, ketchup and mustard. Then stir in the garlic and lemon zest. Season with salt and pepper, then add the lemon juice and hot sauce, if using, to taste.

To assemble the po boys, partially cut the baguettes open lengthways without cutting all the way through. Generously spread each baguette with the sauce, then layer in the lettuce, tomatoes, scampi and gherkins, if using.

# CHOCOLATE CHIP COOKIES

MAKES 12

VEGETARIAN

PREP
15 MINUTES

COOK
15 MINUTES

100g caster sugar
100g soft light brown sugar
240g plain flour
1 tsp baking powder
¼ tsp salt
**200g Heinz [Seriously Good]
Mayonnaise**
1 tsp vanilla extract
100g chocolate, roughly
chopped (use dark, milk
or white chocolate, or a
mixture, depending on
what you like best)

Preheat the oven to 180°C/160°C fan/gas mark 4 and line two baking trays with baking paper.

In a large bowl, mix together both sugars, along with the flour, baking powder and salt. Stir until there are no lumps of sugar left. Add the mayonnaise, vanilla extract and chocolate chunks. Beat together to form a cookie dough – it will look crumbly at first, but will soon come together.

Using clean hands divide the dough into 12 balls. Place these on the lined baking trays, leaving enough room between them to allow for spreading. Bake for 10–12 minutes until the cookies are golden, their edges are set and their centres are still a little soft. Leave to cool on the trays for at least 5 minutes before eating.

*Once baked these cookies will keep happily in an airtight container for 3–4 days.*

# PICNIC

Everyone loves a picnic – it's the perfect way to
get outdoors and enjoy time with friends and
family. And a brilliant excuse to try some tasty
new foods! Forget about limp sandwiches
and soggy salads, though. This chapter is like
a picnic basket bursting with tasty treats,
from Coronation Cauliflower to Potato &
Pea Samosas. There are even BLT Baps, to
really take your picnic game to the next
level – whatever the weather!

MAKES 18

VEGAN

PREP
30 MINUTES

COOK
45 MINUTES

6 sheets of vegan filo pastry
6 tbsp olive oil
1 tbsp nigella seeds

*For the filling*
250g new potatoes, any
    larger ones halved
150g frozen peas
2 spring onions, finely sliced
2.5cm piece of fresh ginger,
    peeled and finely grated
1 fat garlic clove, finely
    grated
1 tbsp garam masala
**2 tbsp Heinz [Seriously
Good] Vegan Mayonnaise,
plus extra to serve**
salt and pepper

*You will need a pastry brush*

# POTATO &
# PEA SAMOSAS

To make the filling, put the potatoes into a saucepan of cold salted water over a medium–high heat. Bring to the boil, then cook for 12–15 minutes until completely tender. Drain and leave to steam dry for a few minutes, then tip into a large bowl.

Roughly mash the potatoes, then stir in the frozen peas, along with the spring onions, ginger, garlic, garam masala and vegan mayonnaise. Season to taste, then set aside to cool. The filling can be made up to a day in advance and kept in the fridge.

When you're ready to bake, preheat the oven to 180°C/160°C fan/gas mark 4 and line two baking trays with baking paper.

Unravel a sheet of filo pastry on to a chopping board, covering the other sheets with a damp tea towel. Brush the pastry with olive oil, then slice lengthways into three strips.

Spoon 1 heaped tbsp of the filling into the top right-hand corner of each pastry strip. Fold the top left-hand corner of the pastry diagonally over the filling to create a triangle, then continue to fold the pastry diagonally over itself until the whole strip of pastry has been used up and you have a sealed samosa. Place on the lined baking tray and repeat.

Brush the samosas with the remaining olive oil and sprinkle over the nigella seeds. Bake for 15–20 minutes until deep golden. Leave to cool for a few minutes before serving with some extra vegan mayo on the side.

# CORONATION CAULIFLOWER

SERVES 4

VEGAN

PREP
10 MINUTES

COOK
20 MINUTES

2 medium cauliflowers, cut into large florets and stalks roughly chopped
1 tbsp medium curry powder
2 tsp cumin seeds
2 tbsp rapeseed oil
salt and pepper

*For the coronation sauce*
**6 tbsp Heinz [Seriously Good] Vegan Mayonnaise**
2 tbsp mango chutney
1 tsp medium curry powder
50g sultanas (optional)
4 spring onions, finely sliced
50g toasted flaked almonds
small bunch of coriander, roughly chopped (stalks and all)

Preheat the oven to 220°C/200°C fan/gas mark 7.

On your largest roasting tray, toss the cauliflower with the curry powder, cumin seeds, rapeseed oil and plenty of salt and pepper, then spread it out into a single layer so that it roasts evenly. Roast for 15–20 minutes until the cauliflower is cooked but still has a slight bite. Set aside to cool slightly.

Meanwhile, make the coronation sauce. In a large bowl, mix together the vegan mayonnaise, mango chutney and curry powder. Add the sultanas, if using, along with most of the spring onions, flaked almonds and coriander. Scrape in the cooled cauliflower, along with all the bits from the tray. Gently fold everything together until the cauliflower is coated in the sauce.

Top with the remaining spring onions, almonds and coriander to serve.

SERVES 4

VEGETARIAN

PREP
15 MINUTES

COOK
20 MINUTES

# BROCCOLI PESTO PASTA SALAD

1 head of broccoli, cut into florets and stalk roughly chopped)

300g pasta of your choice (we like fusilli, farfalle or penne)

100g toasted flaked almonds

small bunch of basil (stalks and all)

1 small garlic clove, peeled

4 tbsp olive oil

zest and juice of 1 lemon

salt and pepper

**6 tbsp Heinz [Seriously Good] Mayonnaise**

60g rocket

200g frozen peas, defrosted

*You will need a food processor*

Bring a large saucepan of salted water to the boil over a medium–high heat and add the broccoli. Cook for 5 minutes until completely soft, then, using a slotted spoon, scoop the broccoli out of the pan and place in a bowl of cold water. This will cool it immediately, which helps the broccoli retain its vivid green colour.

Drop the pasta into the pan of broccoli water and cook according to the packet instructions.

Meanwhile, drain the cooled broccoli, then transfer to a food processor. Add half the almonds, along with the basil, garlic, olive oil, and lemon zest and juice. Blitz until smooth, adding a little water if needed until you have a drizzling consistency. Season to taste. This is your pesto.

When the pasta is cooked, drain, then tip into a large bowl.

Add the broccoli pesto and mayonnaise to the warm pasta and give everything a good toss to coat. Once the pasta is cool, stir through the rocket, peas and remaining flaked almonds. Season to taste.

*This pasta salad will happily keep in the fridge for a couple of days. Best eaten at room temperature.*

*Pictured overleaf.*

# SUMMERY GIANT COUSCOUS

SERVES 16

VEGETARIAN

PREP
15 MINUTES

COOK
10 MINUTES

200g giant couscous

4 carrots, peeled and coarsely grated

200g radishes, finely sliced

4 spring onions, finely sliced

50g toasted pine nuts

50g sultanas

large bunch of mixed herbs (we like parsley, mint and dill), roughly chopped

**20 sprays Heinz Salad Dressing Spray Balsamic with Garlic**

salt and pepper

Cook the giant couscous according to the packet instructions, then drain into a sieve and rinse under cold water until cool.

Tip the cooled couscous into a large bowl. Add the carrots, radishes, spring onions, pine nuts, sultanas and herbs. Give everything a good mix to combine.

Spray in the balsamic dressing, stir and season to taste before serving.

*You can try different vegetables in this salad, depending on what you like.*

*Pictured overleaf.*

SERVES 4

VEGETARIAN

PREP
15 MINUTES

COOK
10 MINUTES

# TRUFFLE EGG MAYO SANDWICHES

6 large free-range eggs

**4 tbsp Heinz [Seriously Good] Truffle Mayonnaise**

1 banana shallot, finely chopped

1 punnet of salad cress, snipped

salt and pepper

8 thick slices of granary bread

4 handfuls of salted crisps

Place a large saucepan of water over a medium–high heat and bring to the boil. Lower in the eggs and set a timer for 7 minutes. Once the timer beeps, use a slotted spoon to transfer the eggs to a bowl of ice-cold water and set aside to cool.

Once the eggs are cool, peel them and place in a large bowl. Add the truffle mayonnaise and roughly mash together using a fork. Stir in the chopped shallot and most of the cress. Season with salt and lots of black pepper to taste.

Divide the egg mayo between four slices of granary bread and top with the crisps for a little crunch. Scatter over the remaining cress. Sandwich together with the remaining bread to serve.

# HONEY & MUSTARD BAKED HAM

SERVES 6–8

PREP
5 MINUTES
PLUS COOLING

COOK
1 HOUR
45 MINUTES

1.25–1.5kg unsmoked
   gammon joint
1 onion, halved
2–3 bay leaves
1 tbsp peppercorns

*For the glaze*
**4 tbsp Heinz Honey Yellow
   Mustard**
50g soft light brown sugar

Put the gammon, onion, bay leaves and peppercorns in your largest saucepan, then pour in enough cold water to cover the gammon. Place over a medium–high heat and bring the water to the boil. Skim off any white froth that has risen to the surface, then reduce the heat to low and gently simmer for 45 minutes (for the smaller size) to 1 hour (for a larger joint). Top up with more water as needed – you want the gammon to be covered in water at all times.

Preheat the oven to 200°C/180°C fan/gas mark 6 and line a large roasting tray with kitchen foil.

Using tongs and a big spoon, lift the gammon out of the liquid and on to the lined roasting tray. Set aside until cool enough to handle. Discard the liquid.

Meanwhile, make the glaze by stirring together the mustard and brown sugar in a small bowl.

Once the gammon is cool enough to handle, remove any strings wrapped around it and take off the outer layer of skin, so that you're left with a layer of fat. Discard the skin. Using a small, sharp knife, score the fat in a criss-cross pattern.

Brush half the glaze over the gammon. Roast for 15 minutes, then spoon over the caramelised juices. Brush with the remaining glaze and roast for another 15 minutes until sticky and deeply caramelised.

Leave to cool, then cut into slices.

*The cooked ham will keep well, wrapped, in the fridge for a week.*

SERVES 4–6

PREP
15 MINUTES
PLUS CHILLING

# PICNIC LOAF

1 small round rustic white loaf

**4 tbsp Heinz [Seriously Good] Mayonnaise**

zest of 1 lemon

black pepper

150g Comté cheese, thinly sliced

150g roasted peppers from a jar, drained and thinly sliced

150g chargrilled artichokes from a jar, drained

80g Parma ham or Italian salami

60g rocket

150g sundried tomatoes, drained

The day before you want to serve this, cut the top off the loaf, then use your hands to hollow out the inside of the bread, removing the doughy centre. (The bread you remove from the centre can be kept, roasted until dry, then blitzed into breadcrumbs to use in another recipe, such as the Four Quarters Mac 'n' Cheese on page 152.)

In a small bowl, mix together the mayonnaise and lemon zest, and season with black pepper. Spread the lemon mayonnaise across the bottom of the hollowed-out loaf, then add the Comté, followed by the roasted peppers, artichokes, Parma ham, rocket and sundried tomatoes, adding each one in a layer. Place the 'lid' back on the loaf, then wrap everything very tightly in clingfilm. Transfer to the fridge and place a couple of tins on top of the loaf to weigh it down overnight.

When you're ready to serve, unwrap the loaf and cut into thick slices or wedges.

# PLOUGHMAN'S SANDWICH

SERVES 4

PREP
15 MINUTES

4 tbsp Heinz [Seriously Good] Mayonnaise

2 tsp Heinz Mild Yellow Mustard

2 large baguettes

4 tbsp Heinz Ploughman's Pickle

100g ham (we like it finely sliced)

100g extra-mature Cheddar, sliced

2 apples, cored and sliced

2 large handfuls of watercress

Mix together the mayonnaise and mustard in a small bowl.

Halve the baguettes so that you have four, then slice each in half lengthways. Spread the mustard mayonnaise across the bottom half of each baguette, and spread the ploughman's pickle across the top half.

Layer the ham, sliced Cheddar, apple and watercress on the bottom half of each baguette, then top with the top halves to complete the sandwiches.

SERVES 6

PREP
30 MINUTES
PLUS CHILLING

COOK
20 MINUTES

# BARBECUE SCOTCH EGGS

8 pork sausages (500g in total)

**2 tbsp Heinz Classic Barbecue Sauce**

**1 tsp Heinz Mild Yellow Mustard**

salt and pepper

100g plain flour, plus extra for dusting

8 medium free-range eggs (6 hard-boiled and peeled, 2 raw)

150g panko breadcrumbs

vegetable oil, for deep-frying

**Heinz Tomato Ketchup, to serve**

*You will need a digital thermometer, if you have one*

Squeeze the sausage meat out of the skins and into a large bowl. Add the barbecue sauce and mustard. Season, then mix it all together using clean hands. Divide into six equal pieces and place them on a plate.

Lightly flour your hands and place one piece of sausage meat in your palm. Flatten into a round patty large enough to encase an egg, then pop one of the peeled boiled eggs in the middle of the patty. Shape the meat around the egg until it is completely sealed. Place on a baking tray and repeat with the remaining meat and eggs. Place in the fridge for 20 minutes to chill.

Breading time! Measure the flour into a small bowl and season with salt and pepper. Crack the remaining two eggs into a second bowl and whisk with a fork to combine. Put the breadcrumbs in a third bowl.

Take the first meat-coated egg from the tray and dip it in the flour to coat, shaking off any excess, then coat it completely in the whisked egg, and finally in the breadcrumbs. Place the breaded scotch egg back on the tray and repeat with the rest.

Fill a deep saucepan two-thirds full with vegetable oil and place over a high heat. Heat the oil to 160°C. Alternatively, check if the oil is ready by dropping a breadcrumb into the pan: it should brown within 40 seconds. Line a second baking tray with baking paper.

Working in batches, deep-fry the scotch eggs for 4–5 minutes until deeply golden, cooked through and crisp. Transfer to the lined tray, then sprinkle with salt. Eat warm or cold, with ketchup for dipping.

# BLT BAPS

SERVES 4

PREP
10 MINUTES

COOK
10 MINUTES

12 slices of back bacon (we like smoked)

2 tsp sherry or red wine vinegar

2 large vine tomatoes, sliced into rounds

salt and pepper

4 large soft white baps (buns), halved

**4 tbsp Heinz [Seriously Good] Garlic & Caramelised Onion Mayonnaise**

1 baby gem lettuce, leaves separated

Preheat the grill to high and line a grill pan or baking tray with kitchen foil.

Lay the bacon slices on the grill pan or tray. Grill for 2–4 minutes on each side, depending on how crispy you like your bacon.

In a small bowl, drizzle the vinegar over the tomatoes and season with salt and pepper.

Spread the bottom of each bap with the mayonnaise, and put three rashers of bacon into each bap. Top with the baby gem lettuce leaves and seasoned tomatoes, then sandwich together with the tops of the baps and serve.

*Pictured overleaf.*

MAKES 8

VEGETARIAN

PREP
15 MINUTES

COOK
15 MINUTES

# BRIE & PICKLE TURNOVERS

500g block of puff pastry
plain flour, for dusting
**4 tbsp Heinz Piccalilli Pickle**
  **or Heinz Ploughman's**
  **Pickle**
150g brie, cut into 8 equal
  pieces
1 medium free-range egg
1 tbsp cold water
1 tbsp poppy seeds

*You will need a rolling pin and*
  *a pastry brush*

Preheat the oven to 200°C/180°C fan/gas mark 6 and line two baking trays with baking paper.

On a floured surface, roll the pastry block into a rectangle measuring roughly 25 x 30cm, and about 5mm thick. Cut the rectangle in half, then cut each half into four quarters, so that you end up with eight small rectangles in total.

Spread ½ tablespoon of the piccalilli in the centre of each pastry square, then top each one with a piece of brie.

Crack the egg into a small bowl, then add the water and whisk with a fork to combine. Brush the egg wash around the outsides of each pastry square, then fold each square over the filling on the diagonal to create eight triangular turnovers. Use a fork to crimp the edges to seal.

Transfer the turnovers to the lined baking trays and brush the tops with the egg wash, then scatter over the poppy seeds. Use a sharp knife to create a small steam hole in the top of each turnover.

Bake for 10–15 minutes until deep golden brown. Swap the position of the trays halfway through so that they cook evenly. Leave to cool a little before serving.

*You can freeze the turnovers before baking and then cook from frozen – just give them an extra 5 minutes. Once cooked, they will keep happily in the fridge for 1–2 days. Bring to room temperature to eat, or, if eating warm, reheat in a hot oven for a few minutes.*

# CAPRESE TARTLETS

SERVES 8

VEGETARIAN

PREP
15 MINUTES

COOK
20 MINUTES

1 small garlic clove, finely
   grated
**5 tbsp Heinz Tomato Ketchup**
1 tbsp balsamic vinegar
plain flour, for dusting
500g block of puff pastry
400g ripe tomatoes, sliced
   (you need 24 slices)
salt and pepper
2 tbsp olive oil, plus extra to
   serve
150g mozzarella ball, torn
handful of basil leaves

*You will need a rolling pin and
   a 9cm round cutter*

Preheat the oven to 200°C/180°C fan/gas mark 6 and line a large baking tray with baking paper.

In a small bowl, mix together the garlic, ketchup and balsamic vinegar, then set aside.

On a floured surface, roll out the pastry block into a rectangle measuring roughly 25 x 30cm, and about 5mm thick. Using a 9cm round cutter, cut out eight circles.

Transfer the pastry circles to the lined baking tray. Leaving a 1cm border around the edge, spread a spoonful of the garlicky ketchup across the bottom of each. Arrange three overlapping slices of tomato on each tart, keeping within the border.

Season the tomatoes with salt and pepper, and drizzle over the olive oil. Bake the tartlets for 15–20 minutes until puffed up and golden.

Divide the mozzarella equally between the tartlets, then top each one with a couple of basil leaves. Drizzle with a little more olive oil to serve.

# CHICKEN NOODLE SALAD

200g rice noodles

150g cooked chicken, shredded

1 cucumber, peeled into long ribbons

2 carrots, peeled into long ribbons

100g sugar snap peas, cut in half lengthways

large handful of coriander, roughly chopped (stalks and all)

large handful of mint, leaves picked

handful of roasted salted peanuts, roughly chopped (optional)

*For the dressing*

juice of 1 lime

2 tbsp peanut butter (crunchy or smooth is fine)

1½ tbsp soy sauce

**3 tbsp Heinz Thai Style Sweet Chilli Sauce**

1 tbsp water

*You will need a blender*

Cook the rice noodles according to the packet instructions, then drain into a sieve and run under cold water until cool.

Meanwhile, make the dressing. In a large bowl, mix together the lime juice, peanut butter, soy sauce, sweet chilli sauce and water.

Tip the cooled rice noodles into the dressing bowl. Add the shredded chicken, cucumber and carrot ribbons, sugar snap peas and most of the herbs. Give everything a good toss to combine.

Scatter with the remaining herbs and chopped peanuts, if using, to serve.

SERVES 4

VEGETARIAN

PREP
10 MINUTES

COOK
5 MINUTES

# WALDORF SALAD

**100g Heinz [Seriously Good] Vegan Mayonnaise**

**1 tbsp Heinz Mild Yellow Mustard**

zest and juice of 1 lemon

100g walnuts, toasted and roughly chopped

4 celery stalks, sliced

200g seedless red grapes, halved

2 apples, cored and chopped

2 baby gem lettuces, leaves separated and core chopped

salt and pepper

In a large bowl, mix together the vegan mayonnaise and mustard with the lemon zest and juice. Add the walnuts, celery, grapes, apples and chopped lettuce core. Toss well until everything is combined. Season with salt and pepper to taste.

Lay the baby gem lettuce leaves at the bottom of a serving plate or salad bowl and pile the rest of the salad on top. If you're out on a picnic, the leaves can be used to scoop up the salad.

# CHEESE TWISTS

SERVES 8

VEGETARIAN

PREP
20 MINUTES

COOK
15 MINUTES

2 x 320g sheets ready-rolled
   puff pastry
**2 tbsp Heinz Mild Yellow
   Mustard**
**3 tbsp Heinz Tomato Ketchup**
200g extra-mature Cheddar,
   finely grated
1 medium free-range egg
1 tbsp cold water
generous sprinkle of dried
   Italian mixed herbs

Preheat the oven to 200°C/180°C fan/gas mark 6 and line two large baking trays with baking paper.

Unravel the sheets of puff pastry and arrange them so that the shorter sides are closest to you. Spread the mustard over the bottom half of the first sheet of pastry, and spread the ketchup over the bottom half of the second sheet. Sprinkle 180g of the grated cheese equally over the top of both sauces.

Fold the empty top halves of pastry over the filled bottoms, pressing down all over to seal. Using a sharp knife, cut each one into eight strips, then, using clean hands, twist each strip of pastry with your fingers so that you end up with a cheesy twist.

Lay the cheesy twists on the lined baking trays, leaving space between each one so they can spread.

Crack the egg into a small bowl and add the water. Whisk with a fork to combine. Brush the egg wash over the cheese twists, then sprinkle over the remaining 20g Cheddar and the Italian herbs. Bake for 12–15 minutes until crisp and deeply golden brown, swapping the position of the trays halfway through so that they cook evenly. Leave to cool before eating.

*The cheese twists will happily keep for 3–4 days in an airtight container.*

# BARBECUE

Barbecues are the perfect way to spend a summer afternoon, although the recipes in this chapter are so tasty you might be tempted to fire up the coals in the middle of winter. Invite over friends and family and cook up Blue Cheese Buffalo Wings, Pork & Pineapple Skewers and the showstopping Ultimate Cheeseburger. There are also truly delicious Sticky Portobello Mushroom Burgers and brilliant sides, including Honey & Mustard Griddled Lettuce and our Best Ever Potato Salad.

SERVES 4

VEGETARIAN

PREP
5 MINUTES

COOK
15 MINUTES

# STICKY PORTOBELLO MUSHROOM BURGERS

**3 tbsp Heinz Sweet & Spicy Barbecue Sauce, plus extra to serve**

1 tbsp water

4 large portobello mushrooms, stems trimmed

1 tbsp olive oil

salt and pepper

4 smoked cheese slices

4 burger buns, halved

**4 tbsp Heinz [Seriously Good] Vegan Garlic Aioli**

1 baby gem lettuce, leaves separated

1 large vine tomato, sliced into rounds

½ red onion, peeled and finely sliced

Preheat the barbecue to high, or place a griddle pan or frying pan over a high heat.

In a small bowl, mix together the barbecue sauce and water.

Rub the mushrooms with the olive oil and season on all sides with salt and pepper. Place the mushrooms on the barbecue, or in the pan. Cook for 4 minutes on each side, then spoon over some of the barbecue sauce mixture. Continue to cook for a couple of minutes, repeatedly glazing the mushrooms in the sauce until they are sticky and caramelised.

Lay a cheese slice over each mushroom. Cover with the barbecue hood or a lid, then cook for a further 30 seconds until the cheese has melted. Transfer to a plate.

Toast the buns, cut-side down for 30 seconds on the barbecue or in the pan, then assemble the burgers.

Spread the aioli on the bottom halves of the buns. Top with the lettuce, sticky mushrooms, tomato slices and red onion, then sandwich together with the bun tops. Serve with more barbecue sauce, if you like.

SERVES 4

VEGETARIAN

PREP
10 MINUTES

COOK
10 MINUTES

# ELOTES-STYLE CORN WITH FETA & CHILLI

4 corn on the cob

**4 tbsp Heinz [Seriously Good] Mayonnaise**

200g feta, crumbled

1 lime, zested, then cut into 4 wedges

1–2 tsp chilli powder (depending on how spicy you like it), plus extra to serve

2–3 tbsp water

1 tbsp olive oil

salt and pepper

*You will need a blender*

Place a large saucepan of salted water over a medium–high heat and bring to the boil. Drop in the corn and cook for 4 minutes, then drain into a colander.

Meanwhile, put the mayonnaise in a blender with 150g of the feta, along with the lime zest, chilli powder and water. Blitz into a smooth sauce and spoon into a wide, shallow bowl.

Preheat the barbecue, or place a frying pan over a high heat.

Drizzle the corn with the olive oil and season with salt and pepper. Lay on the hot barbecue or in the pan and cook for 5–6 minutes, turning regularly until nicely charred, then immediately transfer to the mayonnaise mixture. Using tongs, turn the cobs to evenly coat the corn on all sides.

Lay the coated corn on a plate and spoon over the remaining sauce, then crumble over the rest of the feta and sprinkle with a little more chilli powder. Serve with the lime wedges for squeezing.

*Pictured overleaf.*

# BLUE CHEESE BUFFALO WINGS

SERVES 4

PREP
15 MINUTES

COOK
35 MINUTES

1kg chicken wings, cut in half
at the joint
salt and pepper

*For the buffalo sauce*
75g salted butter
**3 tbsp Heinz Tomato Ketchup**
2 tbsp hot sauce
1 tbsp white wine vinegar
1 small garlic clove, crushed

*For the blue cheese dressing*
**6 tbsp Heinz [Seriously
Good] Mayonnaise**
small handful of chives,
snipped
50g stilton, crumbled

Preheat the barbecue to high, or preheat the oven to 200°C/180°C fan/gas mark 6.

Pat the chicken wings completely dry with some paper towels – this will keep them crisp. Season generously with salt and pepper.

Lay the wings on the barbecue or divide between two roasting trays, making sure to keep space between each one. If cooking on the barbecue, cook for 20–25 minutes, turning frequently. If roasting in the oven, cook for 30–35 minutes, flipping halfway.

Meanwhile, make the sauces. For the buffalo sauce, melt the butter in a small saucepan over a medium heat. Add the ketchup, hot sauce, white wine vinegar and garlic. Whisk together to create a smooth sauce. Season to taste, then set aside, keeping it warm.

For the blue cheese dressing, simply mix together the mayonnaise, chives and stilton in a small bowl. Season to taste.

Once the wings are cooked, transfer them to a large bowl and pour over the buffalo sauce. Toss well so every wing is coated.

Serve the wings with the blue cheese dip and paper towels for sticky fingers.

*Pictured overleaf.*

SERVES 4

PREP
15 MINUTES
PLUS MARINATING

COOK
10 MINUTES

# PORK & PINEAPPLE SKEWERS

thumb-sized piece of fresh
ginger, peeled and finely
grated

**4 tbsp Heinz Korean Style
Sticky Barbecue Sauce**

1 tbsp rice wine vinegar

500g pork tenderloin, cut
into 2.5cm long strips

salt and pepper

½ very ripe pineapple, peeled
and cut into 2.5cm chunks

bunch of spring onions, cut
into 2.5cm long pieces

kimchi, to serve (optional)

*You will need 8 metal or
wooden skewers (if using
wooden skewers, soak in
hot water for 30 minutes
before using)*

In a large bowl, mix together the ginger, barbecue sauce and rice wine vinegar. Add the pork, then season with salt and pepper. Mix well so that each slice of pork gets coated in the marinade. Cover and chill for at least 1 hour, or up to overnight if feasible.

Once marinated, thread the pork, pineapple and spring onion on to eight skewers, alternating between each one.

Preheat the barbecue to high, or place a griddle pan or frying pan over a high heat.

Cook the skewers for 3–5 minutes on each side, basting with the marinade while they cook, until the pork is cooked through and everything is sticky and caramelised.

Serve the skewers with kimchi, if you like.

SERVES 4

PREP
15 MINUTES
PLUS CHILLING

COOK
10 MINUTES

# LAMB KOFTAS

500g lamb mince
2 tbsp baharat or shawarma
   spice mix
salt and pepper
1 tbsp olive oil

*For the salad*
200g cherry tomatoes,
   halved
1 small red onion, finely
   chopped
1 cucumber, chopped
1 tsp dried mint
1 tbsp red wine vinegar

*To serve*
pickled chillies
toasted flatbreads
**Heinz Turkish Style Garlic
   Sauce**

Tip the lamb mince into a large bowl. Add the baharat or shawarma spice mix, along with plenty of salt and pepper. Using clean hands, knead the spices evenly throughout the meat, then shape the lamb into 12 finger-length, roughly oval-shaped koftas. Transfer to a baking tray, then cover and chill for 20 minutes.

For the salad, mix together the tomatoes, red onion, cucumber, dried mint and red wine vinegar in a large bowl. Season with salt and pepper to taste.

When you're ready to cook, preheat the barbecue to high, or place a large griddle pan or two large frying pans over a high heat.

Drizzle the koftas with the olive oil, then lay on the barbecue or in the pan(s). Flatten slightly with a fish slice, then cook for 2–3 minutes on each side until cooked through and caramelised. Pile on to a plate.

Serve the koftas with the salad, along with some pickled chillies, toasted flatbreads and lots of garlic sauce.

# BEST-EVER POTATO SALAD

SERVES 4–6

VEGETARIAN

PREP
10 MINUTES

COOK
15 MINUTES

750g new potatoes (we like Jersey Royals), any larger ones halved

salt and pepper

**5 tbsp Heinz [Seriously Good] Mayonnaise**

**5 tbsp Heinz Salad Cream**

8 cornichons, finely chopped

2 tbsp capers, drained

handful of dill, chopped

handful of chives, snipped

Put the new potatoes in a large saucepan of cold salted water over a medium–high heat. Bring to the boil, then cook for about 12–15 minutes until the potatoes are tender and a sharp knife slides into the centre easily. Drain into a colander and leave to steam dry.

In a large bowl, stir together the mayonnaise and salad cream. Add the warm potatoes, along with the cornichons and capers. Give everything a good mix to combine. Stir through the herbs and season the potato salad to taste.

*This potato salad tastes even better the next day, so why not get ahead for your barbecue and make it in advance?*

# CHICKEN THIGHS WITH AJI VERDE

1 tbsp olive oil
8 skin-on, bone-in chicken
 thighs
salt and pepper
2 limes, halved

*For the aji verde*
small bunch of coriander
 (stalks and all)
1 small garlic clove, peeled
**4 tbsp Heinz [Seriously
 Good] Mayonnaise**
6–8 pickled jalapeño slices
 (depending on how spicy
 you like it), plus 2 tbsp
 pickling juice from the jar

*You will need a food processor*

Preheat the barbecue to high, or preheat the oven to 220°C/200°C fan/gas mark 7.

Rub the olive oil over the chicken thighs and season well with salt and pepper. Lay the chicken thighs skin-side down on the barbecue, or, if cooking in the oven, place on a roasting tray skin-side up. If cooking on the barbecue, cook for 30 minutes, turning occasionally. If cooking in the oven, roast for 40 minutes. For the final 5 minutes, place the limes, cut-side down, on the barbecue or roasting tray. Cook alongside the chicken, until charred.

Meanwhile, make the aji verde. Put all the ingredients in a food processor and blitz to form a smooth green sauce. Season to taste.

Serve the chicken drizzled with the aji verde, with the charred limes for squeezing over.

# HALLOUMI & COURGETTE BURGER

SERVES 4

VEGETARIAN

PREP
15 MINUTES

COOK
25 MINUTES

2 courgettes, diagonally
    sliced
2 tbsp olive oil
salt and pepper
**2 tbsp Heinz Tomato Ketchup**
1 tsp chilli powder
450g halloumi, cut into thick
    strips
4 seeded burger buns, halved
**4 tbsp Heinz [Seriously
    Good] Mayonnaise**
4 handfuls of watercress
8 sundried tomatoes, drained

*You will need a pastry brush*

Preheat the barbecue to high, or place a griddle pan or frying pan over a high heat.

In a large bowl, toss the courgettes in the olive oil and season with salt and pepper. Lay the courgette slices on the barbecue or in the pan (you may need to do this in two batches). Cook for 3–4 minutes on each side until charred, then tip back into the bowl. Set aside.

In a small bowl, mix together the tomato ketchup and chilli powder.

Place the halloumi strips on the barbecue or in the pan. Cook for 2 minutes until crisp and golden, then flip, brush with the spicy ketchup and cook for another 2 minutes. Once sticky and glazed, transfer to a plate.

Toast the buns, cut-side down, on the barbecue or in the pan for 30 seconds.

Spread the mayonnaise across the bottom halves of the buns, then top with the watercress, followed by the halloumi, sundried tomatoes and courgettes. Sandwich together with the bun tops to serve.

# ULTIMATE CHEESEBURGER

SERVES 4

PREP
10 MINUTES
PLUS CHILLING

COOK
15 MINUTES

500g beef mince (the best
   quality you can afford)
**1 tbsp Heinz Tomato Ketchup**
salt and pepper
8 burger cheese slices
4 brioche buns, halved
½ head of iceberg lettuce,
   shredded
2 gherkins, sliced

*For the burger sauce*
**1 tbsp Heinz Tomato Ketchup**
**3 tbsp Heinz [Seriously
   Good] Mayonnaise**
**1 tbsp Heinz Mild Yellow
   Mustard**
1 banana shallot, very finely
   chopped
1 gherkin, very finely chopped,
   plus 1 tbsp pickling juice
   from the jar

Tip the beef mince into a large bowl. Add the tomato ketchup and season with plenty of salt and pepper, then, using clean hands, mix together and shape into four large burger patties. Cover and chill in the fridge while you make the burger sauce.

In a bowl, mix together all the burger sauce ingredients and season to taste. Set aside.

Preheat the barbecue to high or place a frying pan over a high heat.

Place the burger patties on the barbecue or in the pan. Flatten slightly with a fish slice and season with salt. Fry for 2 minutes on each side until crisp and caramelised, then lay over the cheese slices. Cover (with the barbecue hood or a lid) and cook for a further 30 seconds until the cheese has melted. Transfer to a plate.

Toast the brioche rolls, cut-side down, for 30 seconds on the barbecue or in the frying pan, then assemble the burgers.

Spread half the burger sauce across the lower halves of the rolls. Top each one with a cheeseburger and some iceberg lettuce and sliced gherkins, then spoon over the remaining burger sauce. Sandwich together with the tops of the rolls.

*If you're short on time, you can just use Heinz American Style Burger Sauce.*

# TRIPLE ONION HOT DOGS

4 jumbo hot dogs

**2 tbsp Heinz [Seriously Good] Garlic & Caramelised Onion Mayonnaise**

4 large hot dog rolls, split down the middle

**squirt of Heinz Mild Yellow Mustard**

2 tbsp ready-made crispy onions

*For the caramelised onions*
2 large onions, finely sliced
250ml water
2 tbsp olive oil
salt
**1 tbsp Heinz Tomato Ketchup**
½ tbsp balsamic vinegar

To make the caramelised onions, place the onions in a saucepan over a medium heat. Pour in the water and cook for 20 minutes or so until all the water has evaporated and the onions have collapsed.

Increase the heat to high and add the olive oil and a good pinch of salt. Fry, stirring regularly, for 10–15 minutes, until the onions are beginning to caramelise, then stir through the ketchup and balsamic vinegar. Cook for a further 5 minutes until sticky and golden, then set aside and keep warm. (The caramelised onions can be made the day before and kept in the fridge overnight – just reheat before use.)

Preheat the barbecue to high, or place a large griddle pan or frying pan over a high heat. Lay on the jumbo hot dogs and cook, turning regularly, for 8–10 minutes until cooked through and nicely charred in places.

Spread the mayonnaise across the bottom half of each hot dog roll, then spoon in some caramelised onions and place a hot dog on top. Squirt over some mustard and top with the crispy onions to serve.

SERVES 4–6

VEGETARIAN

PREP
5 MINUTES

COOK
5 MINUTES

# HONEY & MUSTARD GRIDDLED LETTUCE

2 tbsp olive oil
4 baby gem lettuces, halved
salt and pepper
50g mixed seeds, toasted
big pinch of dried chilli flakes

*For the dressing*
2 tbsp olive oil
1 tbsp white wine vinegar
**2 tsp Heinz Honey Yellow
  Mustard**
zest and juice of ½ lemon

In a small bowl, whisk together the dressing ingredients and season to taste. Set aside.

Preheat the barbecue to high, or place a large griddle pan or two large frying pans over a high heat.

Brush the olive oil over the cut side of the lettuce halves and season well with salt and pepper. Place the lettuce halves on the barbecue or in the pan(s), cut-side down. Cook for 3–5 minutes until nicely charred and beginning to collapse and soften.

Transfer the lettuce halves to a plate and place them cut-side up. Spoon over the dressing. Scatter over the mixed seeds and a big pinch of chilli flakes to serve.

# SMOKY AUBERGINE & POMEGRANATE

SERVES 4

VEGETARIAN
(VEGAN OPTION)

PREP
10 MINUTES

COOK
30 MINUTES

3 large aubergines

**2 tbsp Heinz Turkish Style Garlic Sauce**

2 tbsp olive oil, plus extra to serve

zest and juice of 1 lemon

1 tbsp tahini (optional)

salt and pepper

2 tbsp pomegranate seeds

50g walnuts, toasted and roughly chopped (optional)

flatbreads, to serve (try our Easy Garlic Flatbreads on page 149)

Preheat the barbecue or grill to high.

Prick the aubergines all over with a sharp knife, then place on the barbecue or under the grill. Cook, turning occasionally, until collapsed and blackened. This will take about 20 minutes on the barbecue, or about 30 minutes in the oven – you want to char the outside completely. Once charred, set aside to cool.

Once the aubergines are cool, use clean fingers to remove their blackened skin – don't worry if a few flecks of skin get left behind, this will just add to the smoky flavour. Place the aubergine flesh in a large bowl.

Add the garlic sauce, olive oil, lemon zest and juice and tahini, if using. Roughly mash everything together with a fork, then season with salt and pepper to taste.

Spoon the aubergine mixture into a serving bowl. Drizzle over a little more olive oil, then top with the pomegranate seeds and walnuts, if using. We like to serve these with our Easy Garlic Flatbreads, for dipping.

*Make this vegan by replacing the Heinz Turkish Style Garlic Sauce with 2 tablespoons of Heinz [Seriously Good] Vegan Garlic Aioli.*

*Pictured overleaf.*

# CREAMY COLESLAW

**5 tbsp Heinz [Seriously Good] Mayonnaise**

100ml double cream

**2 tsp Heinz Mild Yellow Mustard**

1 small white cabbage, very finely sliced

4 carrots, peeled and coarsely grated

1 white onion, very finely sliced

salt and pepper

In a large bowl, whisk together the mayonnaise, double cream and mustard. Add the cabbage, carrot and onion. Using clean hands, massage well so that all the veg gets coated in the dressing and begins to soften, then season with salt and pepper to taste.

*This can be made a few hours in advance and kept covered in the fridge.*

*This is delicious with the Ultimate Cheeseburger on page 141.*

# EASY GARLIC FLATBREADS

SERVES 4

VEGAN

PREP
25 MINUTES

COOK
15 MINUTES

300g self-raising flour, plus
    extra for dusting
1 tsp salt
**50g Heinz [Seriously Good]**
    **Vegan Garlic Aioli**
2 tbsp olive oil, plus extra to
    serve
150ml water
good pinch of za'atar
    (optional)

*You will need a rolling pin*

Stir the flour and salt together in a large bowl. Add the vegan aioli and olive oil, then pour in the water. Mix until you have a shaggy dough.

Tip the dough out on to a floured surface and, using clean hands, knead for 5 minutes until smooth. Cover the dough with a clean tea towel and leave to rest for 15 minutes.

Cut the dough into eight equal pieces, then shape each piece into a ball. On a floured surface, roll the dough balls into oval flatbreads about 5mm thick. Keep the prepared flatbreads and the rest of the dough balls covered while you roll out each flatbread.

Preheat the barbecue to high, or place a griddle pan or frying pan over a high heat.

Cook the flatbreads in batches on the barbecue, or one at a time in the pan, for 1–2 minutes on each side until puffed up, golden and nicely charred in places.

Serve warm, brushed with a little more olive oil and sprinkled with za'atar if you like.

*These flatbreads are best eaten as soon as they are made, and are perfect served with the Smoky Aubergine & Pomegranate on page 145.*

# KIDS' PARTY

Next time you host a kids' party, break out these brilliant recipes and nobody will be disappointed. Sneak in some veg with the Four Quarters Mac 'n' Cheese and Hidden Veg Toasties, and let the kids serve themselves with creative DIY Veggie Fajitas. For a super-easy option, there are Ciabatta Pizza Slices. And no party would be complete without cake – we've got that covered, too.

# FOUR QUARTERS MAC 'N' CHEESE

50g diced pancetta

1 small onion, finely chopped

100g button mushrooms, halved

1 small garlic clove, crushed

2 tbsp dried breadcrumbs

1 tbsp olive oil

salt and pepper

1 red pepper, finely chopped

big pinch of dried chilli flakes

100g frozen sweetcorn, defrosted

**4 x 400g tins Heinz Macaroni Cheese**

30g Cheddar, grated

handful of tortilla chips, crushed

100g cherry tomatoes, halved

100g frozen peas

2 tbsp green pesto

Preheat the oven to 200°C/180°C fan/gas mark 6.

Tip the pancetta into a frying pan over a medium–high heat and fry, stirring occasionally, for 5 minutes until crisp. Using a slotted spoon, remove the pancetta from the pan and transfer to a bowl, leaving the cooking juices behind. Keep the frying pan over the heat and add the onion and mushrooms. Cook, stirring regularly, for 6–8 minutes until both are golden, then scrape into the bowl with the pancetta.

In a small bowl, mix together the garlic, breadcrumbs and olive oil, and season with salt and pepper. In a separate small bowl, mix together the red pepper, chilli flakes and sweetcorn.

Tip the macaroni cheese into a rectangular baking dish and spread it in an even layer. Imagine the top is divided into four quarters. Spoon the pancetta mix across the top of one quarter, and sprinkle over the Cheddar. Spoon the sweetcorn and peppers across the second quarter, then sprinkle over the crushed tortilla chips. Top the third quarter with the cherry tomatoes, then scatter over the garlicky breadcrumbs. This will leave one quarter free, which you'll top later.

Bake for 15–20 minutes until bubbling and golden brown.

Once the macaroni is cooked, place the peas in a microwavable bowl and microwave on high for 2 minutes. Stir the pesto through the peas, then top the final quarter of the macaroni with the pesto peas. Bring the mac 'n' cheese to the table to serve.

# CIABATTA PIZZA SLICES

SERVES 6

VEGETARIAN OPTION

PREP
15 MINUTES

COOK
15 MINUTES

2 ciabatta loaves, sliced in
half lengthways
2 tbsp olive oil
1 fat garlic clove, crushed
**8 tbsp Heinz Tomato Ketchup**
1 tsp dried oregano
1 orange pepper, finely sliced
6–8 sundried tomatoes,
drained
12 slices of pepperoni
(optional)
250g mozzarella, torn

Preheat the oven to 220°C/200°C fan/gas mark 7.

Lay the ciabatta halves, cut-side up, on a wire rack set over a roasting tin. Drizzle over the olive oil.

In a small bowl, mix together the garlic, ketchup and oregano: this is your pizza sauce. Spread this mixture evenly across the bread. Top with the pepper, sundried tomatoes and pepperoni, if using, then scatter over the mozzarella.

Bake in the oven for 10–12 minutes until the mozzarella has melted and the ciabatta is crisp. Leave the pizza to cool a little, then cut into finger slices to serve.

*You can swap out the pepper for other veggies.*

# SUPER-CRISPY TUNA MELTS

2 x 160g tins sustainably
   sourced tuna, drained
198g tin sweetcorn, drained
2 spring onions, finely sliced
**6 tbsp Heinz [Seriously
   Good] Mayonnaise**
salt and pepper
8 thick slices of crusty bread
1 tbsp olive oil
150g Cheddar, grated

Tip the tuna into a large bowl. Add the sweetcorn, spring onions and 4 tablespoons of the mayonnaise. Stir together and season with salt and pepper.

Spread the remaining mayonnaise across one side of the bread slices.

Pour ½ tablespoon of the olive oil into a large frying pan over a medium–high heat. Lay two slices of bread in the pan, mayonnaise-side down – this is the secret to an extra-crispy toastie.

Spoon a quarter of the tuna mayonnaise over each slice, then top each with a quarter of the grated Cheddar. Sandwich together with two more bread slices, mayonnaise side facing up.

Fry the tuna melts for 2–3 minutes on each side, using a fish slice to squash the sandwiches together while they cook. Once melting and crisp, remove to a plate and repeat with the remaining oil, bread, tuna mayo and Cheddar.

Cut the tuna melts into squares to serve.

# HIDDEN VEG TOASTIES

SERVES 4–6

VEGETARIAN

PREP
10 MINUTES

COOK
20 MINUTES

2 tbsp olive oil

1 small onion, finely chopped

1 red pepper, cut into small cubes

1 small sweet potato, peeled and cut into small cubes

salt and pepper

**400g tin Heinz Spaghetti Hoops**

2 tsp unsalted butter

8 slices of white bread

150g Cheddar, grated

Heat the olive oil in a saucepan over a medium heat. Add the onion, red pepper and sweet potato. Season with a little salt and pepper and cook, stirring occasionally, for 10–12 minutes until the veg is soft.

Tip in the spaghetti hoops and stir to warm through, then take off the heat.

Melt 1 teaspoon of butter in a toastie maker. Lay in two slices of bread. Spread a quarter of the spaghetti hoop mixture across each slice, then top each with a quarter of the grated Cheddar. Sandwich together with two more bread slices. Toast according to the machine instructions, then repeat with the remaining ingredients to make two more toasties.

Cut each toastie into four triangles to serve.

*If you don't have a toastie maker, you can cook the toasties for 2 minutes on each side in a hot frying pan in a little melted butter.*

SERVES 6

VEGETARIAN

PREP
10 MINUTES

COOK
15 MINUTES

# DIY VEGGIE FAJITAS

2 tbsp olive oil

2 onions, finely sliced

2 peppers (any colour), finely sliced

1–2 tbsp fajita seasoning (depending on how spicy you like it)

175g baby corn, halved lengthways

**3 tbsp Heinz Tomato Ketchup**

2 tbsp water

salt and pepper

12 small flour or corn tortillas

2 avocados, sliced

½ romaine lettuce, finely sliced

100g Cheddar, grated

*For the salsa*

200g cherry tomatoes, quartered

1 pepper, finely chopped

**1 tbsp Heinz Tomato Ketchup**

juice of 1 lime

pinch of dried chilli flakes (optional)

Heat the olive oil in a large frying pan over a medium–high heat. Add the onions and sliced peppers and cook, stirring regularly, for 6–8 minutes until collapsed and softened.

Add the fajita seasoning and baby corn to the pan. Give everything a good stir to coat in the spices, then spoon in the tomato ketchup and water. Mix and season to taste, then reduce the heat to medium and leave to simmer away while you make the salsa.

To make the salsa, mix together the tomatoes and finely chopped pepper in a small bowl, then add the ketchup and lime juice. Give everything a good mix, then add the chilli flakes, if using, and season the salsa with salt and pepper to taste.

Heat the tortillas according to the packet instructions.

Serve the fajita filling alongside the salsa, sliced avocados, lettuce, Cheddar and tortillas, so that everyone can assemble their own fajitas.

*You can swap the peppers for any veggies you like.*

# PEPPER & PANEER SKEWERS

SERVES 6

VEGETARIAN

PREP
15 MINUTES

COOK
10 MINUTES

2 red peppers, cut into
chunks
450g paneer, cut into large
cubes
1 broccoli head, cut into
florets
1 tbsp olive oil
salt and pepper

*For the sweet chilli sauce
glaze*
1 tbsp olive oil
**3 tbsp Heinz Thai Style
Sweet Chilli Sauce**

*You will need 12 small wooden
skewers (soak in hot water
for 30 minutes before using)*

Mix together the peppers, paneer and broccoli in a large bowl. Add the olive oil and season with salt and pepper. Give everything a good toss to combine.

To make the sweet chilli sauce glaze, mix together the olive oil and sweet chilli sauce in a small bowl.

Preheat the grill to high and line a grill pan or large roasting tray with kitchen foil.

Thread the peppers, paneer and broccoli on to 12 skewers, alternating between each one. Lay the skewers on the lined pan or roasting tray. Grill for 5 minutes on each side, basting regularly with the sweet chilli sauce glaze, until everything is nicely browned and the veg has softened.

Serve and enjoy.

*If your kids don't like peppers or broccoli, you could try making these with courgettes, mushrooms or aubergines.*

SERVES 6

PREP
10 MINUTES
PLUS CHILLING

COOK
15 MINUTES

# BARBECUE CHICKEN NUGGETS

285ml buttermilk

**2 tbsp Heinz Classic Barbecue Sauce, plus extra to serve**

4 chicken breasts, cut into small nugget-sized pieces

salt and pepper

200g fine dried breadcrumbs

2 tbsp olive oil

**Heinz Tomato Ketchup, to serve**

In a large bowl, mix together the buttermilk and barbecue sauce. Add the chicken, season with salt and pepper, and mix well so that each piece of chicken gets coated in the marinade. Cover and chill for at least 1 hour, or up to overnight if feasible.

When you're ready to cook, preheat the oven to 220°C/200°C fan/gas mark 7 and line a large roasting tray with baking paper. Pour the breadcrumbs into a wide, shallow bowl.

Working in batches, shake any excess buttermilk mixture off the chicken pieces, then coat completely in the breadcrumbs. Transfer to the lined tray, and repeat until you've breaded all the chicken nuggets.

Drizzle the nuggets with the olive oil, then roast for 15 minutes until cooked through and golden brown.

Serve with more barbecue sauce and ketchup, for dipping.

*It's fun to serve these with carrot sticks and cucumber batons for a finger-food feast.*

*Pictured overleaf.*

# SMASHED NEW POTATOES

SERVES 6

VEGETARIAN

PREP
5 MINUTES

COOK
40 MINUTES

750g new potatoes,
    kept whole
3 tbsp olive oil
salt

*To serve*
**Heinz [Seriously Good]
    Vegan Garlic Aioli
Heinz Tomato Ketchup
Heinz Classic Barbecue
    Sauce**

Preheat the oven to 220°C/200°C fan/gas mark 7.

Put the new potatoes into a large saucepan of cold salted water over a medium–high heat. Bring to the boil, then cook for 8 minutes. Drain into a colander and leave to steam dry.

Tip the potatoes into your largest roasting tray, then, using a fish slice, press down on each one to flatten and lightly smash. Drizzle over the olive oil and season with salt.

Roast the smashed potatoes for 25–30 minutes, flipping halfway, until completely crisp and golden brown.

Serve with the vegan garlic aioli, tomato ketchup and barbecue sauce for dipping.

*Pictured overleaf.*

# LOADED CHORIZO NACHOS

1 tbsp olive oil

225g chorizo, peeled and diced

1½ red onions, very finely chopped

2 orange peppers, finely chopped

1 tsp smoked paprika

2 tsp ground cumin

**2 x 415g tins Heinz Five Beanz**

salt and pepper

400g tortilla chips

150g grated mozzarella

*To serve*

4 tbsp soured cream

½ red onion, very finely chopped

handful of coriander, roughly chopped (stalks and all)

2 avocados, diced

Heat the olive oil in a large frying pan over a medium–high heat. Add the chorizo, red onions and peppers. Cook, stirring regularly, for 5–6 minutes until the veg has collapsed and the chorizo has released its oils.

Add the smoked paprika and cumin to the pan. Give everything a good mix, then tip in the beans. Stir and allow to simmer away for a few minutes. Season to taste.

Preheat the grill to high.

Tip the tortilla chips into a large roasting tin and spread out in an even layer. Spoon over the chorizo and bean filling, then evenly scatter over the grated mozzarella. Slide under the grill for 2–3 minutes until the cheese has melted and everything is bubbling and golden.

Leave the nachos to cool a little, then spoon over the soured cream. Top with the red onion, coriander and avocado to serve.

*If you know your kids won't like raw red onion, then just add all the onion to the chorizo at the beginning. It will still be delicious.*

SERVES 4–6

PREP
5 MINUTES

COOK
25 MINUTES

# HONEY & MUSTARD CHIPOLATAS

12 chipolata sausages

2 tsp olive oil

**2 tbsp Heinz Honey Yellow Mustard**

Preheat the oven to 180°C/160°C fan/gas mark 4 and line a roasting tray with kitchen foil.

Arrange the chipolatas on the lined roasting tray. Roast for 20 minutes, flipping once.

Meanwhile, mix together the olive oil and mustard in a small bowl.

Increase the oven temperature to 200°C/180°C fan/gas mark 6.

Spoon the mustard mixture over the chipolatas, then return to the oven for 5 minutes until sticky and caramelised. Serve with your favourite sauce for dipping.

# CHOCOLATE CUPCAKES

SERVES 10

VEGETARIAN

PREP
15 MINUTES

COOK
15 MINUTES

100g self-raising flour
50g cocoa powder
75g caster sugar
75g soft light brown sugar
pinch of salt (optional)
2 medium free-range eggs
**150g Heinz [Seriously Good]**
 **Mayonnaise**
1 tsp vanilla extract
50ml boiling water

*For the icing*
100g soft unsalted butter
200g icing sugar
2 tbsp cocoa powder
1 tbsp milk

*You will need a cupcake tray,*
 *10 cupcake cases and an*
 *electric whisk*

Preheat the oven to 180°C/160°C fan/gas mark 4 and line a cupcake tray with 10 cupcake cases.

In a large bowl, whisk together the flour, cocoa powder and both sugars, along with a pinch of salt, if using. Crack in the eggs and add the mayonnaise and vanilla extract, then whisk to a smooth cake batter. Pour in the boiling water – this is the secret ingredient for an extra-fudgy chocolate cake – and whisk well until fully combined.

Spoon the cake batter into the cupcake cases. Bake in the centre of the oven for 12–15 minutes until the cakes are well risen, and a skewer inserted into the centre of a cupcake comes out clean. Set aside to cool on a wire rack.

To make the icing, use an electric whisk to beat the butter in a bowl until it is super light in colour, then add the icing sugar and cocoa powder. Whisk to create a smooth chocolate buttercream. Pour in the milk and whisk again to combine.

Spoon or pipe the buttercream on to the cooled cupcakes and serve.

*The iced cupcakes will keep for up to 5 days in an airtight container. You can also freeze the un-iced cupcakes, well wrapped. Defrost thoroughly and then add the icing to serve.*

SERVES 12

VEGETARIAN

PREP
20 MINUTES

COOK
25 MINUTES

# VANILLA PARTY SHEET CAKE

200g self-raising flour

200g caster sugar

¼ tsp salt

3 medium free-range eggs

**200g Heinz [Seriously Good] Mayonnaise**

2 tsp vanilla extract

50ml milk

*For the frosting*

70g soft unsalted butter, plus a little extra for greasing

180g cream cheese

300g icing sugar

1 tsp vanilla extract

2 tbsp rainbow sprinkles

*You will need a 20 x 20cm springform brownie tin and an electric whisk*

Preheat the oven to 180°C/160°C fan/gas mark 4. Grease a 20 x 20 cm springform brownie tin with butter and line the base with baking paper.

In a large bowl, whisk together the flour, sugar and salt. Crack the eggs into a separate bowl. Add the mayonnaise, vanilla extract and milk to the eggs, and whisk to combine.

Pour the wet ingredients into the dry and whisk well until you have a smooth vanilla cake batter. Spoon the batter into the prepared tin, and smooth out the top using the back of a spoon so that it's even.

Bake in the centre of the oven for 20–25 minutes until the cake is well risen and lightly golden, and a skewer inserted into the centre comes out clean. Set aside to cool for 10 minutes in its tin, then transfer to a wire rack to cool completely.

To make the frosting, use an electric whisk to beat the butter with the cream cheese in a large bowl until smooth. Add the icing sugar and vanilla extract, and whisk to create a smooth frosting.

Spread the frosting over the cooled vanilla cake, then scatter over the rainbow sprinkles. Cut into 12 squares to serve.

# WEEKEND FEASTS

After a busy week, the weekend gives us the chance to slow down and unwind, so these recipes are all about celebrating that with a tasty family feast. Whether you're inviting friends over, or just have time to create something a bit special, you're sure to find inspiration here. The Spatchcock Chicken & Charred Cabbage is perfect for a special occasion, while the Mediterranean-Style Baked Feta makes an ideal centrepiece. For a summer lunch, try the Easiest Ever Gazpacho with Salsa Verde & Croutons – followed by a tempting slice of Summer Berry Sponge.

# CAMPECHANA
## (MEXICAN-STYLE PRAWN COCKTAIL)

1 large avocado, halved

juice of 1 lime

**400g carton Heinz Tomato, Roasted Garlic and Black Pepper Soup, chilled overnight in the fridge**

1 red onion, finely chopped

100g green olives, pitted and chopped

1–2 jalapeño chillies (depending on how spicy you like it), finely chopped

**4 tbsp Heinz Tomato Ketchup**

salt and pepper

300g sustainably sourced peeled and cooked king prawns

handful of coriander, chopped (stalks and all)

Cut half of the avocado into cubes and slice the other half. Squeeze over a little of the lime juice and set aside.

Pour the cold soup into a large bowl. Add the red onion, olives, jalapeño(s) and ketchup. Give everything a good mix to combine. Add the remaining lime juice and season the sauce with salt and pepper to taste.

Save six of the cooked prawns for the top of the cocktail, then fold the rest through the sauce, along with the cubed avocado and coriander.

Spoon the mixture into four glasses. Top each with one of the remaining prawns and the slices of avocado, fanned at the side of each glass.

# CHARRED STEAK
## WITH CRUNCHY PEANUT SALAD

SERVES 4

PREP
20 MINUTES

COOK
5 MINUTES

2 x 225g sirloin steaks
1 tbsp rapeseed oil
salt and pepper
**2 tbsp Heinz Thai Style Sweet Chilli Sauce**

*For the crunchy peanut salad*
**3 tbsp Heinz Thai Style Sweet Chilli Sauce**
3 tbsp fish sauce
juice of 2 limes
1 small red cabbage, very finely sliced
1 cucumber, cut into matchsticks
200g radishes, finely sliced
100g roasted salted peanuts, roughly chopped
large handful of mint, leaves picked
large handful of coriander, roughly chopped (stalks and all)

Take the steaks out of the fridge half an hour before you begin cooking so that they come up to room temperature.

When you're ready to cook, rub the steaks with the rapeseed oil, then season generously on both sides with salt and pepper. Spread out the sweet chilli sauce on a plate.

Place a large frying pan over a high heat until searingly hot, then lay the steaks in the pan. Fry to your liking (2 minutes on each side for medium–rare). Once cooked, remove the steaks from the pan with tongs and transfer to the plate with the sweet chilli sauce, turning them to coat on both sides. Leave the steaks to rest on the plate while you assemble the salad.

For the salad, mix together the sweet chilli sauce, fish sauce and lime juice in a large bowl. Add the cabbage, cucumber, radishes, peanuts, mint and coriander. Toss the salad well to combine.

Cut the rested steak into diagonal strips. Divide the salad and steak strips between four plates to serve, spooning over the resting juices from the steaks.

SERVES 4

PREP
15 MINUTES
PLUS RESTING

COOK
1 HOUR

# SPATCHCOCK CHICKEN & CHARRED CABBAGE

1 free-range chicken (about
    1.3–1.5kg)
1 tbsp olive oil
salt and pepper

*For the charred cabbage*
    *salad*
2 small pointed (sweetheart)
    cabbages, quartered
    lengthways
2 tbsp olive oil
**4 tbsp Heinz Salad Cream**
30g Parmesan, finely grated
2 tbsp capers, roughly
    chopped
small handful of parsley,
    roughly chopped (stalks
    and all)
50g toasted hazelnuts,
    roughly chopped

Preheat the oven to 220°C/200°C fan/gas mark 7.

To spatchcock the chicken, lay it on a chopping board, breast-side down. Starting from the leg end, use sharp kitchen scissors to cut down either side of the back bone, then remove. Flip the chicken over and press gently on the breast to flatten the chicken.

Transfer the spatchcocked chicken, breast-side up, to a large roasting tray. Drizzle over the olive oil and season generously all over with salt and pepper. Roast for 40–45 minutes until golden, crisp and cooked through – the juices should run clear when you cut into the thickest part of the thigh. Once cooked, leave to rest for 15–20 minutes.

When the chicken has 15 minutes left in the oven, prepare the cabbage. Lay the cabbage quarters, cut-side down, on a roasting tray. Drizzle over the olive oil and season with salt and pepper. Roast for 25–30 minutes, flipping halfway, until cooked through and charred.

Pile the roasted cabbage on to a large platter and drizzle over the salad cream. Top with the grated Parmesan, capers, parsley and toasted hazelnuts. Carve the chicken and arrange on another platter, then pour over its resting juices. Serve both together in the middle of the table.

*Pictured overleaf.*

# TRUFFLE & PANCETTA POTATO SKINS

SERVES 4

PREP
10 MINUTES

COOK
1 HOUR
15 MINUTES

4 baking potatoes (we like King Edwards), scrubbed
salt and pepper
100g diced pancetta
1 tbsp olive oil
small bunch of chives, snipped
**4 tbsp Heinz [Seriously Good] Truffle Mayonnaise**
100g Gruyère cheese, finely grated

Preheat the oven to 200°C/180°C fan/gas mark 6.

Prick the potatoes all over with a sharp knife. Place on a baking tray and sprinkle with salt and pepper. Bake for 45 minutes–1 hour until cooked through.

Meanwhile, tip the pancetta into a frying pan over a medium–high heat. Fry, stirring occasionally, for 5 minutes until crisp, then tip into a large bowl.

Once the potatoes are cooked, set aside to cool slightly and increase the oven temperature to 220°C/200°C fan/gas mark 7.

Once the potatoes are cool enough to handle, cut each one in half lengthways. Scoop out the soft middles into the bowl with the pancetta, and put the potato skins back on the baking tray. Drizzle the skins with olive oil and season with a little more salt and pepper, then return them to the oven for 5 minutes to crisp up.

While the skins are crisping, add most of the chives and all the truffle mayonnaise to the bowl with the potato insides and pancetta. Give everything a good mix and season to taste.

Stuff the potato and pancetta filling into the crisped potato skins, then scatter over the grated Gruyère. Roast for a further 8–10 minutes until the cheese has melted and the stuffed potato skins are bubbling and golden.

Sprinkle over the remaining chives to serve.

SERVES 4

PREP
15 MINUTES

COOK
25 MINUTES

# WHOLE BAKED SEA BASS

2 sustainably sourced whole sea bass (about 500g), cleaned

salt and pepper

5cm piece of fresh ginger, peeled and cut into matchsticks

4 spring onions, cut into matchsticks

**4 tbsp Heinz Thai Style Sweet Chilli Sauce**

300g Jasmine rice

handful of coriander, leaves picked

1 lime, cut into wedges

stir-fried greens, to serve (see below)

Preheat the oven to 200°C/180°C fan/gas mark 6 and line a large roasting tray with kitchen foil.

Season the sea bass inside and out with salt and pepper, then lay on the lined roasting tray. In a small bowl, mix together the ginger and spring onions, then use half of this mixture to stuff both sea bass. Roast the sea bass in the oven for 15 minutes, then remove and spoon over the sweet chilli sauce. Return to the oven and roast for a further 10 minutes until cooked through, sticky and caramelised – the fish should come off the bone easily.

While the sea bass are roasting, rinse and cook the rice according to the packet instructions.

Transfer the roasted sea bass to a large platter and scatter over the remaining ginger and spring onion mixture, along with the coriander. Serve with the rice, lime wedges and some stir-fried greens and let everyone help themselves.

*For easy stir-fried greens, heat 2 tablespoons of sesame oil in a large frying pan over a high heat. Add a handful each of sliced pak choi, mangetout and green beans. Fry for 3–4 minutes until the pak choi has wilted. Season with soy sauce to taste.*

# FISH STEW

SERVES 4

PREP
10 MINUTES

COOK
45 MINUTES

2 tbsp olive oil

1 large fennel bulb, sliced, green fronds reserved

1 tsp dried chilli flakes

1 tsp fennel seeds

3 fat garlic cloves, finely sliced

250ml white wine

**2 x 400g tins Heinz Cream of Tomato Soup**

500g mussels or clams, cleaned

salt and pepper

2 sustainably sourced firm white fish fillets (about 120g; we like hake), cut into medium chunks

8 sustainably sourced shell-on king prawns

**4 tbsp Heinz Mediterranean Style Aioli Sauce or Heinz [Seriously Good] Vegan Garlic Aioli**

small handful of parsley, roughly chopped (stalks and all)

1 lemon, cut into 4 wedges

crusty baguette, to serve

Heat the olive oil in a large saucepan over a medium–high heat. Add the sliced fennel and cook, stirring regularly, for 8–10 minutes until softened and beginning to caramelise.

Add the chilli flakes, fennel seeds and garlic to the pan. Cook, stirring, for 1 minute, then pour in the white wine. Once the wine has reduced by half, add the tomato soup. Stir and bring to a simmer, then let it bubble away for 10 minutes.

Meanwhile, check that the mussels or clams are clean. Throw away any shells that are open and won't shut when you press them together in the palm of your hand. Season the fish with salt and pepper.

Add the mussels or clams, white fish and prawns to the sauce. Cover the pan with a lid and cook for 5 minutes until all the shells have opened, the fish is cooked through and the prawns have turned from grey to pink. Season the fish stew to taste.

Ladle the stew into four bowls. Top with the aioli, then sprinkle over the parsley and reserved fennel fronds. Serve with the lemon wedges for squeezing, and a crusty baguette.

# JALAPEÑO & CORN CRAYFISH ROLLS

**4 tbsp Heinz [Seriously Good] Mayonnaise**
**2 tbsp Heinz Tomato Ketchup**
8 pickled jalapeños, 4 finely chopped and 4 kept whole
zest and juice of ½ lemon
198g tin sweetcorn, drained
200g sustainably sourced crayfish tails (or small Atlantic prawns)
salt and pepper
4 hot dog rolls
small handful of chives, snipped (optional)

In a large bowl, mix together the mayonnaise, ketchup, finely chopped pickled jalapeños and lemon zest and juice. Add the sweetcorn and crayfish tails and give everything a good mix to combine. Season with salt and pepper to taste.

Warm the hot dog rolls for a few minutes in a low oven, then split down the middle, making sure not to cut them completely in half. Fill each roll with the crayfish mixture, then top with the remaining pickled jalapeños and chives, if using, to serve.

# CHEESE, ARTICHOKE & SPINACH DIP

SERVES 6

VEGETARIAN OPTION

PREP
15 MINUTES

COOK
20 MINUTES

2 garlic cloves, crushed

**350g Heinz [Seriously Good] Mayonnaise**

2 x 280g jars artichokes, drained and roughly chopped

zest of 1 lemon

150g chopped frozen spinach, defrosted and drained

100g Parmesan or vegetarian hard cheese, grated

150g Cheddar, grated

black pepper

tortilla chips and crudités, to serve

Preheat the oven to 180°C/160°C fan/gas mark 4.

In a large bowl, mix together the garlic, mayonnaise, artichokes, lemon zest and spinach. Add most of the grated Parmesan and Cheddar, and stir to combine. Season with lots of black pepper.

Transfer the mixture into a small baking dish and spread it out into an even layer, then top with the remaining grated cheeses. Bake for 20 minutes until bubbling, cheesy and golden brown.

Leave to stand for 5 minutes before eating. Serve with tortilla chips and crudités of your choice, for dipping.

# PISTACHIO & PARSLEY CRUSTED HAKE

50g pistachios, chopped

4 tbsp panko breadcrumbs

zest and juice of 1 lemon

1 tbsp olive oil

bunch of parsley, chopped
(stalks and all)

salt and pepper

4 sustainably sourced hake
fillets (about 120g), skin
left on

**6 tbsp Heinz [Seriously
Good] Mayonnaise**

1 tbsp cumin seeds

2 fennel bulbs, very finely
sliced

Preheat the oven to 200°C/180°C fan/gas mark 6. Line a roasting tray with baking paper.

In a small bowl, mix together the pistachios, breadcrumbs, lemon zest and olive oil, along with half of the parsley. Season with salt and pepper.

Season the hake fillets all over with salt and pepper, then lay skin-side down on the lined roasting tray. Spread 1 tablespoon of the mayonnaise across the top of each fish fillet, then top with the pistachio breadcrumbs, patting to stick the breadcrumbs to the fish. Roast for 8–10 minutes until the fish is cooked through but still moist.

Meanwhile, toast the cumin seeds in a dry frying pan over a medium heat for about 30 seconds until fragrant. Transfer to a bowl and add the sliced fennel and lemon juice, along with the remaining 2 tablespoons of mayonnaise and the rest of the parsley. Toss to combine, then season the salad to taste.

Serve the crusted hake alongside the fennel and cumin seed salad.

# EASIEST EVER GAZPACHO
## WITH SALSA VERDE & CROUTONS

SERVES 4

VEGETARIAN

PREP
10 MINUTES
PLUS CHILLING

COOK
5 MINUTES

3 x 400g tins Heinz Cream
of Tomato Soup, decanted
into a large bowl or jug
and chilled overnight in the
fridge

*For the croutons*
2 tbsp olive oil
3 thick slices of sourdough,
cut into large chunks
(crusts left on)
salt and pepper

*For the salsa verde*
4 tbsp olive oil
large handful of parsley,
finely chopped (stalks and
all)
1 tbsp red wine vinegar
**2 tsp Heinz Mild Yellow
Mustard**
2 tbsp capers, roughly
chopped
zest and juice of ½ lemon

To make the croutons, heat the olive oil in a large frying pan over a medium–high heat. Add the sourdough bread chunks and season well with salt and pepper. Fry, turning regularly using tongs, for 4–5 minutes until evenly golden and crisp. Remove from the heat and set aside.

To make the salsa verde, mix all the ingredients together in a bowl. Season to taste.

To serve, divide the chilled soup between four bowls. Top each with a generous swirl of the salsa verde and a scattering of croutons.

SERVES 4

VEGETARIAN

PREP
10 MINUTES

COOK
10 MINUTES

# SUMMERY PESTO GNOCCHI

salt and pepper

200g green beans, trimmed

500g fresh gnocchi

150g fresh green vegetarian pesto

**6 tbsp Heinz [Seriously Good] Mayonnaise**

400g cherry tomatoes, halved

3 tbsp capers

60g rocket

Bring a large saucepan of salted water to the boil over a medium–high heat. Add the green beans and cook for 3–4 minutes until just tender. Remove with a slotted spoon and transfer to a large bowl, keeping the saucepan on the heat.

Drop the gnocchi into the water and cook according to the packet instructions – the gnocchi are ready when they begin to float. Drain, then tip into the bowl with the green beans.

Spoon the pesto and mayonnaise into the bowl with the gnocchi and beans. Mix well so that everything gets nicely coated in the sauce, then add the cherry tomatoes, capers and rocket. Toss together and season to taste.

# MEDITERRANEAN-STYLE BAKED FETA

SERVES 4

VEGETARIAN

PREP
10 MINUTES

COOK
20 MINUTES

**2 x 400g tins Heinz Cream of Tomato Soup**

**4 tbsp Heinz Tomato Ketchup**

2 tsp smoked paprika

2 x 400g tins chickpeas, drained

salt and pepper

450g jar roasted peppers, drained and roughly sliced

100g garlicky olives, sliced

200g block of feta

1 tbsp olive oil

50g toasted pine nuts

Preheat the oven to 200°C/180°C fan/gas mark 6.

Pour the tomato soup into a large bowl. Add the ketchup and smoked paprika and stir to combine, then tip in the chickpeas. Give everything a good mix, and season with salt and pepper.

Tip the tomatoey chickpeas into a large rectangular baking dish. Mix through the roasted peppers and olives. Place the block of feta in the middle of the dish, then drizzle over the olive oil. Bake for 20 minutes until the feta is beginning to turn lightly golden at the edges.

Scatter over the toasted pine nuts to serve.

*This is delicious served with a simple green salad.*

SERVES 4

VEGETARIAN

PREP
15 MINUTES

COOK
25 MINUTES

# SPICED HALLOUMI PITTA POCKETS

1 tbsp smoked paprika

½ tsp garlic granules

1 tsp dried oregano

1 tsp ground cumin

500g frozen oven chips

1 tbsp olive oil

**3 tbsp Heinz Tomato Ketchup, plus extra to serve**

450g halloumi, thickly sliced

4 large pitta breads

½ cucumber, sliced

½ red onion, finely sliced

**4 tbsp Heinz Salad Cream**

juice of ½ lemon

Preheat the oven to 200°C/180°C fan/gas mark 6.

In a small bowl, mix together the smoked paprika, garlic granules, oregano and cumin. Tip the oven chips on to a large roasting tray and spoon over half the spice mix. Toss together, then spread out in a single layer so that they cook evenly. Bake the chips for 25–30 minutes until golden and crisp, flipping halfway through.

Meanwhile, add the olive oil and tomato ketchup to the remaining spice mix and stir together. Lay the halloumi slices in a small baking dish. Cover with the spiced ketchup mixture. Place in the oven for 15 minutes until the halloumi is turning golden.

Warm the pitta breads in a toaster and slice in half. Stuff each pitta bread with tomatoey halloumi, cucumber, red onion and some of the spiced chips, then drizzle over the salad cream and squeeze over the lemon juice. Serve with the remaining chips and more ketchup, if you like.

# SUMMER BERRY SPONGE

SERVES 8–10

VEGETARIAN

PREP
25 MINUTES
PLUS COOLING

COOK
20 MINUTES

vegetable oil, for greasing
4 medium free-range eggs
200g caster sugar
**200g Heinz [Seriously Good]**
  **Mayonnaise**
1 tsp vanilla extract
200g self-raising flour
1 tsp baking powder
salt

*For the filling*
300ml double cream
1 tbsp caster sugar
1 tsp vanilla extract
150g raspberry jam
200g summer berries, larger
  ones sliced (we like a
  mix of strawberries and
  raspberries)

*To finish*
1 tbsp caster sugar

*You will need 2 x 20cm cake
  tins and an electric whisk*

Preheat the oven to 180°C/160°C fan/gas mark 4. Grease 2 x 20cm cake tins with a little oil and line the bases with baking paper.

Using an electric whisk, beat the eggs and caster sugar in a large bowl until they are super light and fluffy. You want the mixture to double in size. Add the mayonnaise, vanilla extract, flour, baking powder and a pinch of salt. Briefly whisk to create a smooth cake batter.

Divide the batter evenly between the two lined cake tins. Bake in the centre of the oven for 20 minutes, until the cakes are well risen and golden and a skewer inserted into the centre comes out clean. Leave to cool in their tins for 10 minutes, then transfer to a wire rack to cool completely.

Once the cakes are cooled, make the filling. In a large bowl, whisk together the cream, sugar and vanilla extract until the mixture is firm enough to just hold its shape.

Place one of the sponge cakes on a serving plate. Spread the jam across the top of the sponge, then spoon over the double cream mixture. Dot the berries across the top of the cream, then top with the remaining sponge to create a sandwich cake. Sprinkle with caster sugar and serve.

*Although best eaten on the day it is made, this cake will keep in the fridge in an airtight container for 1–2 days.*

SERVES 12

VEGETARIAN

PREP
20 MINUTES

COOK
30 MINUTES

# SALTED CARAMEL HAZELNUT BROWNIES

200g dark chocolate,
  snapped into pieces
3 medium free-range eggs
275g caster sugar
**200g Heinz [Seriously Good]**
  **Mayonnaise**
50g self-raising flour
50g cocoa powder
100g shop-bought salted
  caramel sauce
50g blanched hazelnuts,
  toasted and roughly
  chopped
salt

*You will need a 20 x 20cm*
  *brownie tin and an electric*
  *whisk*

Preheat the oven to 180°C/160°C fan/gas mark 4. Grease a 20cm x 20cm brownie tin with a little oil and line with baking paper.

Put the chocolate in a heatproof bowl and place over a pan of barely simmering water to melt, stirring occasionally. Alternatively, melt the chocolate in the microwave, heating it in 30-second bursts until liquid and glossy.

In a separate large bowl, beat together the eggs and sugar using an electric whisk until they are super light and fluffy. You want the mixture to double in size. Add the melted dark chocolate, along with the mayonnaise, flour and cocoa powder. Whisk until smooth.

Spread half the brownie batter into your lined tin. Swirl over half the caramel sauce, then scatter over half the hazelnuts. Next, spread over the remaining brownie batter in an even layer, then top with the remaining caramel sauce and hazelnuts. Sprinkle over a little salt.

Bake in the centre of the oven for 25–30 minutes until set at the edges but still a little gooey in the centre. Leave to cool in the tin, then cut into 12 squares.

*The brownies will happily keep in an airtight container for up to 5 days. If you like your brownies a little fudgy, keep them in the fridge.*

# INDEX

Published in 2022 by Ebury Press an imprint of Ebury Publishing,
20 Vauxhall Bridge Road,
London SW1V 2SA

Ebury Press is part of the Penguin Random House group of companies
whose addresses can be found at global.penguinrandomhouse.com

The HEINZ trademarks are owned by H.J. Heinz Foods UK Limited
and are used under licence. © 2022 H.J. Heinz Foods UK Limited

Text © Ebury Press 2022
Photography © Ebury Press 2022
Design © Ebury Press 2022

Publishing Director: Elizabeth Bond
Photography: Haarala Hamilton
Design: A2 Creative
Food Styling: Sophie Godwin
Props Styling: Rachel Vere
Writer: Sophie Godwin
Project Editor: Tara O'Sullivan
Development: Heinz New Ventures

www.penguin.co.uk
A CIP catalogue record for this book is available from the British Library
ISBN 9781529148732

Printed and bound in Latvia by Livonia Print SIA

The authorized representative in the EEA is Penguin Random House Ireland,
Morrison Chambers, 32 Nassau Street, Dublin D02 YH68

Penguin Random House is committed to a sustainable future for our business, our readers and
our planet. This book is made from Forest Stewardship Council® certified paper.